Tasting & Touring Michigan's Homegrown Food:

A Culinary Roadtrip

Jaye Beeler

photography by Dianne Carroll Burdick

TASTING & TOURING MICHIGAN'S HOMEGROWN FOOD:

A CULINARY ROADTRIP

BY JAYE BEELER

PHOTOGRAPHY BY DIANNE CARROLL BURDICK

Dianne Carroll Burdick

Arbutus Press ~ Traverse City, Michigan

Printed in China

Arbutus Press
Traverse City, Michigan
info@arbutuspress.com
www.Arbutuspress.com

ISBN 978-1-933926-31-5
Library of Congress Cataloging-in-publication-data

Beeler, Jaye.
 Tasting & touring Michigan's homegrown food:
 a culinary roadtrip / by Jaye Beeler;
photography by Dianne Carroll Burdick.
    p. cm.
 Includes index.
 ISBN 978-1-933926-31-5
1. Food industry and trade—Michigan. 2. Farms, Small-
Michigan. 3. Agritourism—Michigan.
I. Burdick, Dianne Carroll.
II. Title. III. Title:
Tasting and touring Michigan's homegrown food.
 HD9007.M5B44 2012
 381'.4109774--dc23
                                    2011043126

Contents

Acknowledgements 6

Foreword 9

Introduction 15

From the Field 25

From the Orchard 65

From the Water 81

From the Dairybarn 97

From the Barnyard 121

From the Market 137

From the Kitchen 157

Recipes 187

Index 215

SWEET CORN
$5/DOZEN
OR 50¢ EAR
LOCALLY GROWN
AT JOHNECHECK FARM

Acknowledgements
Jaye Beeler

To my husband, Richard Jelier, for introducing me to food that matters in the most far-flung places from South America to Australia, for believing our family table should entertain the purest, local, seasonal ingredients that we can find.

To Dianne Carroll Burdick, for beautifully photographing every aspect of taste-making from the field to the table. Your perfectionism, friendship and culinary sensibilities inspired the best in me.

To Susan Bays, my publisher at Arbutus Press, for believing in this book, making this culinary journey possible and her skill in coordinating such an ambitious project.

To Mark Lewison, at *The Grand Rapids Press*, for generously editing, advising and fact-finding.

To my dad, James Beeler, for his testing and styling of the book's recipes and passing on the culinary gene to my big sister, Quita, and me.

To my food angels: Jacqueline, Natalie and Nicolas, for embracing the interesting fruits and vegetables that I brought home and accompanying me to pastures, fields and farmers market during my fieldwork.

To my mom, Gloria Beeler, and in-laws, Richard and Donna Jelier, for unwavering support and encouragement. Finally, I thank the following for their help: Dianna Stampler/Promote Michigan; Susan Burns and Frits Hoendervanger of Detroit; Lynn Perry and her husband, the late Bill Reed; Luz McCoy; Kristiane and Matt Hubbard, of Grand Rapids; Katie Frank/Zingerman's Bakehouse, Ann Arbor; Karen and Jeff Lubbers/Lubbers Family Farm, Grand Rapids; Randall Fogelman/Eastern Market Corporation, Detroit; Slow Food Potawatomi (Grand Rapids) and Huron Valley (Ann Arbor) convivia; Michigan State University Extension; and those that welcomed us.

Acknowledgements
Dianne Carroll Burdick

My thanks go out to many for making this book possible.

For the opportunity to work with such a fine writer for miles upon miles, thank you to Jaye Beeler.

For making it all happen, I thank Susan Bays of Arbutus Press for creating and maintaining the vision.

For digital imaging, advice, patience and all the Upper Peninsula driving, my deepest appreciation goes to my husband, Rob Burdick. He is my right arm, left brain and wheelman always.

For all the lodging along the way, thank you to Lynn Perry, Chris Byron and Tom Wilson, George and Gretchen Zuiderveen and J. Michael DeAgostino/Grand Traverse Resort.

For the Midas men in Marquette when the car broke down.

For those friends and family along the way who offered support, ideas, and encouragement throughout this project, I thank my mother Shirley Carroll (cat-sitting Baby and Pearl), friends Stephanie Neal (offering pages of places), Julie Christianson Stivers (the road to Romenesco cauliflower), Wendy Marty (Upper Peninsula highlights), and Don Pearson (Big Bay links), and finally, with heartfelt thanks, to all the people of Michigan with their fields, orchards, farms, waterways, kitchens, gardens, businesses, and products that I had the privilege to photograph and document. I learned so much from them and realized that because of them, this book will entertain, educate and enlighten.

7

FOREWORD

Tasting and Touring Michigan's Homegrown Food: A Culinary Roadtrip is all about the succulence of Michigan's homegrown food. For more than a decade, my wife, Jaye Beeler, has set our family table with the delicious bounty of food found in this book. As an award-winning journalist and former food editor of *The Grand Rapids Press*, Jaye brought amazing stories and recipes to her devoted readers. The dishes were beautifully photographed, kitchen-tested in our home, and brimming with local ingredients and flavor. In this new chapter of her journalistic career, Jaye's stories, together with Dianne Carroll Burdick's stunning photography, capture the Michigan local-food scene. They are sure to set your taste buds tingling.

Jaye and Dianne's culinary tour describes the many delightful places in their statewide journey, yet this is also serious business. The economic well-being of our state is critically linked to our land-based industries—of which we are blessed with abundance. If these gifts are squandered, the starter energy that drives our economy will dissipate. As a professor of economic and community development at Grand Valley State University and co-founder of Michigan Higher Education Land Policy Consortium (MIHELP), I was asked by Jaye to address some of the important facts about Michigan—so she can get on with the fun. Building sustainable, local living economies will be a major challenge during this century, especially in the food industry.

The days of the "3,000-mile Caesar salad," made up of foodstuffs shipped from afar, are most likely coming to an end. For the past half-

"The days of the 3,000-mile Caesar salad are over."

century, we have seen economies of scale dominate production. But think of "economies of place" for a moment. A brighter future here, where we live, will necessitate building stronger local economies again, and they can be constructed in part on great food, grown locally, that is fresher and better for your family's health. Over time, those economies of place can trump economies of scale. And this is great news for Michigan's home-grown-food providers.

Building and supporting these local economies is critical to our bottom line. As repeatedly proven by Building Alliances for Local Living Economies (BALLE), spending at a locally owned business on average keeps 68 out of every 100 dollars circulating within the community. When spending on things from outside our communities, however, only 43 dollars stay local.

A 2008 study of Kent County by Civic Economics—commissioned by Local First—determined that just a 10 percent shift in consumer spending toward locally owned businesses would result in an estimated $140 million in new economic activity, 1,600 new jobs,

and $50 million in new wages! If every household started spending just 10 dollars more per week of its current grocery budget on locally grown foods, more than $40 million per week would be kept circulating within Michigan's economy. Let's put it this way: Every dollar spent locally impacts three to seven local businesses before leaving the local economy.

Michigan's land-based industries (agriculture, tourism, forestry, and mining) annually contribute more than $71 billion (29 percent) of Michigan's economic output.

With the decline of manufacturing in Michigan, these land-based industries have eclipsed manufacturing and become the biggest driver of our state economy. Michigan has a total land area of more than 36 million acres. Its farmland is in excess of 10 million acres—or 27 percent of the total land area. Production agriculture, food processing, and related businesses employ approximately one million residents and contribute $15 billion directly to Michigan's economy and another $22 billion indirectly through support and related services. Further,

our unique landscape produces more than 200 commodities, making the state second only to California in terms of crop diversity. A challenge for Michigan is that some of the most productive agricultural land is under threat by poorly planned and uncontrolled development. Ottawa County, west of Grand Rapids, is a prime example. It is Michigan's most productive agricultural county and yet second fastest in terms of overall development as well. When acreage in Michigan is taken out of agricultural production to build subdivisions and shopping districts, it rarely returns to growing food. Yes, areas of Detroit are emerging as urban gardening districts, but the process is long.

Statewide, Michigan lost more than 440,000 acres to development over 10 years, starting in 1987. The Michigan Land Resource Project estimates that developed land will increase by 178 percent by the year 2040. Some parts of the state responded to these pressures on choice agricultural land by establishing Purchase of Development Rights (PDR) programs. Kent County adopted a PDR ordinance in 2002 with the

goal of preserving 25,000 acres by 2013. Due to lack of funding, however, the county has only been able to preserve a little more than 1,000 acres and 11 farms. Old Mission Peninsula has been more successful in using PDR to secure 33 conservation easements, along with the Grand Traverse Regional Land Conservancy, together preserving more than 5,000 acres on the peninsula. On the east side of the state, Ann Arbor voters, in 2003, supported the establishment of a Greenbelt District with a five-mill, 30-year property tax. The Open Space and Parkland Preservation Program is expected to raise at least $87 million to support PDR. Through 2009, the city already has spent slightly more than $10 million on a dozen properties preserving more than 1,321 acres in Washtenaw County.

Farmland preservation efforts must be balanced with programs that support agricultural businesses. In my recent book with Gary Sands, *Sustaining Michigan: Metropolitan Policies and Strategies* (2009, Michigan State University Press), Charles Ballard pointed out that the three state of Michigan departments most associated with land use—agriculture, environmental quality, and natural resources—together make up less than 1 percent of the state's overall operating budget.

The decline of manufacturing from 27 percent of the state's economy in 1963 to about 12 percent in 2006- necessitates rethinking the importance of our land-based industries. We need to preserve agricultural land and adopt smart growth strategies that lessen development pressure on farms. The investment in our local farms described in this book will help support what Michael Schuman has dubbed the "Small-Mart Revolution."

Michigan is at a crossroads, yet there are plenty of reasons to be optimistic. The local-food movement here is strong and getting stronger. In 2008, our annual agricultural exports generated nearly $1.7 billion and employed more than 19,000 residents. Even after all of the tough decades for the family farm, Michigan is home to 56,000 farms averaging 179 acres each.

Now, in recent years, significant growth has occurred in the number of small and large farms in the state. Finally, interest in sustainable development is growing in Michigan—and everywhere. The primary focus of sustainability is on the "triple bottom line" of environmental stewardship, economic prosperity, and social responsibility. Some refer to it as the "Three E's" (economy, environment, equity), while others call it the "Three P's" (profits, planet, people). Whatever you call it, it is clear that this book, *Tasting and Touring Michigan's Home Grown Food,* is consistent with the sustainability principles of the triple bottom line. So, enjoy this Culinary Roadtrip as you take a foodie tour of this wonderful state. If we all start living more locally and authentically, we'll help inspire a new era of prosperity in the state.

Richard W. Jelier, Ph.D.
Professor, School of Public, Nonprofit and Health
Administration
Grand Valley State University

INTRODUCTION

—⁓—

O n a sunny spring day, I am surrounded by
garden greenery and nature's budding bounty.
This scene is the soul-lifting reason I am
visiting this farm. This is a time to take in the beauty
and learn of the bounty.

Pausing under the framework of a humble
greenhouse still under construction, I cradle a carton
of softly bluish eggs laid that morning from Araucana
hens—the breed also known as Easter Egger. Also
cradled is an aromatic armful of Tristar-variety
strawberries, but the proprietor here insists the berries
aren't quite up to her standards and refuses to take
a cent for the beauties. Nearby, a few minutes ago,
young Nubian goats nibbled at me, cottontails from the
"neighborhood" hip-hopped by, and the farm family's
toddler, 3-year-old Hazel, strolled among some potted
fig trees. Three thriving varieties of figs: Peter's Honey,
Vern's Brown Turkey and Black Spanish.

In the yard and gardens of a family-owned,
certified-organic operation in Fennville, just inland from
Lake Michigan, Mari Reijmerink tells me passionately
about Michigan's new breed of agriculturists. She talks
of today's growers who understand that thoughtful,
well-informed agricultural practices are essential. She
talks of farmers who know all sorts of things that many
others—the masses so removed from the land—are
starting to realize might just be life-and-death matters.

Mari Reijmerink and her Netherlands-born
husband, Chris, are small-operation local food producers
who exemplify what *Tasting and Touring Michigan's
Homegrown Food* is all about. To make it in this
endeavor of theirs, they work and work, sometimes
18-hour crunch-time days because the berries are ready

or the chicks are hatching or…it's always something.
But beyond the cash-crop aspect of their livelihood, the
Reijmerinks are on a mission to put the taste back into
food, to help us identify what grows in these parts, and
where and when you can find it at market. Good produce
and other farm goods should be available to everyone,
they say, as a matter of social justice.

The people, the product

On this and many other farm visits, I am witnessing Michigan's flavor frontier: The shift away from factory food and transcontinental shipping to a delight for delicious things right within our grasp. To the harmony of homegrown. To the spirit of sustainable. This Culinary Roadtrip sings the praises of local, seasonal, sustainability raised, and of realigning our lives with those who work our state and regional fields for good food.

We decided to go for it

Early on, seasoned Michigan photographer, Dianne Carroll Burdick and I rambled out to an Oceana County asparagas field—green and gleaming with one of spring's first vegatables. We were inspired by what we saw, and out of that inspiration came this book. I was a longtime food editor for *The Grand Rapids Press,* and Dianne had photographed countless spreads, from recipe shots to banquets, for *The Press* and other publications. In our minds, even before any of the beautiful roadside scenery and savory stops, we could already "taste" the book we would share with you: Great Lakes whitefish blackened to crusty perfection, South Haven peaches so luscious they dribbled when bitten, heirloom tomatoes still warm from the vine and hand-crafted goat cheese so unbelievably tangy-good.

If you seek variety, look about you

Geographically and agriculturally, Michigan is vast and varied, with landscapes that range widely in topography, growing zone, and more. From the better known and more populated southern tier of Michigan cities, a car trip to points north reveals an amazing state. All along the way, the local-food movement is gaining momentum. Many of us are taking matters into our own hands, tracking down delicious produce at markets, roadside stands, and small farms. For this book, our search for Michigan's holy grail of homegrown

connected us to those who value farm products and the hard labor of growers. This tasting tour of the Great Lakes State concentrates on agriculturists with a direct link to the consumer. For the most part, we skipped middlemen and big commercial outlets in favor of Mom and Pop and their small-scale compatriots.

Direct link to you

Exactly who are these Michigan growers who sell from the roadside or a stand at the farmers market? The Lubbers family is a good example. From their land on the Kent/Ottawa county line, Karen Lubbers and her kin attract a lot of city dwellers wanting to know where their food comes from.

"Michigan is so underappreciated as a state, as a beautiful place, as an amazing place to eat..."

Karen says many of her customers begin buying for health reasons, others want to do right by the environment, and then there are the food fanatics, the ones who get light-headed over a pasture-raised fresh turkey, a sugar-pie pumpkin, or an alpine-style aged cheese from a little local dairy. The foodies probably make the best argument, she says. "The first two reasons don't matter a whole lot—after they get a taste of the goodness," she explains.

One of the best ways to go local is through a farmers market. Visit there to find out what's in season, what's in stock, and who's selling it where. Finding local markets has never been easier, too: Michigan now ranks fourth in the nation for the most operational farmers markets, according to the United States Department of Agriculture. In 2010, there were 271 official farmers markets listed in the USDA directory. California claimed the top spot, with 580 official sites, followed by New York, with 461, and Illinois, 286.

Another big step on your food journey is to try something new whenever you confront it. An American heirloom pear called Clapp's Favorite, named for the Massachusetts farmer who developed the mottled, butter-colored pear more than a century ago. Never tried it? Buy it.

How about some thimbleberries, an old-time berry type shaped like a thumb-size thimble? Give 'em a try.

Taste these, too, from Michigan's bounty of local farms:

- a round of LaMancha MOO!
  a Camembert-style, softly ripened cheese made from pasteurized goat's milk at Evergreen Lane Creamery
- eggs from a stylish, plumed Buff Polish chicken
- bacon from a Tamworth heritage pig
- striped heirloom tomato goodness from a variety, Green Zebra, that looks like its name

What a trip

For more than a year, Dianne and I researched the Michigan scene, from a field of thimbleberries to the fishing wharves at Naubinway, in the U.P. From the bustling Eastern Market in Detroit to the Huron-Manistee National Forest (for elusive and yummy morel mushrooms). Acknowledging but looking beyond industrial Michigan and its high jobless rate in the cities, we were looking for the extraordinarily good. It was a quest for the enticing flavors and inviting stories of food, farm and community. Agriculture is a huge part of the Michigan story (the state produces more than 200 edible commodities), ranking second only to California in the variety of crops grown in our nutrient-rich soil. Michigan's agri-food sector generates more than $71 billion annually, making it the state's second largest industry and employing more than one million people.

The local food scene, of course, is only one slice of that big agri-business pie. It might be the most delicious slice, though. Keep in mind, while reading *Tasting and Touring Michigan's Homegrown Food,* that the farms, markets and locally sourced restaurants we encounter are but a fraction of the choices available to you. From wherever you are on The Mitten or above, sniff out your farmers market, sustainable growers, roadside stands, U-pick sites, CSA groups, and more. Discover the homegrown food culture. The way I see it, it's a sumptuous search worth celebrating three times a day—when you eat. Make it something special.

FOODIE FINDS

PICK YOUR OWN at pickyourown.org/MI; divided into counties and regions.

Try the MICHIGAN FARMERS MARKET ASSOCIATION at www.mifma.org for the nearest Michigan farmers markets (estimated at 271.) Click on the 'find a farmers market' link.

REAL TIME FARMS at www.realtimefarms.com, launched in May 2010 by Karl and Cara Rosaen, connects the small-food communities including community supported agriculture, cow shares, micro-creameries, micro-breweries, pesticide-free farms, farmstead restaurants, artisan bakers, chocolatiers and culinarians that work exceedingly hard for your enjoyment. Similar to Wikipedia, Real Time Farms ask enthusiastic eaters to go online, share, educate, edit the descriptions and listings of farms and farmers markets, and contribute photos from the farmers markets they go to and tagging them with the goods available.

Find Real Times Farm at:-
http://twitter.com/realtimefarms
http://facebook.com/realtimefarms
http://realtimefarms.tumblr.com

Join a COMMUNITY SUPPORTED AGRICULTURE (CSA) farm in Michigan at csafarms.org; click on the "Find a CSA" link. Also LOCAL HARVEST at localharvest.org/csa has a searchable database for locating CSAs, farm markets, and other local food options. Join SLOW FOOD, the international movement to promote food grown locally in an environmentally sustainable way, and prepared from scratch at home. Slow Food local chapters help explore the local food scene, host tastings, cooking classes, festivals, films, and farm-to-table dinners.

FROM THE FIELD

—m—

On the first day of spring, we try an early launch for our Culinary Roadtrip of Michigan, but the ground is still frosty white and frozen hard. Close to home, photographer Dianne Carroll Burdick knows of an ancestral maple syrup shack where the steamy sap reducing process unfolds. Her brother has in-laws that own the sugarhouse operation in Byron Center near Grand Rapids where Dianne delivers toasty warm and amber gold photos from here. Soon enough we head for more destinations.

A few of our field destinations:

- The town of Hart in early spring for great green growths of asparagus
- Traverse City for some fabulous cherries
- Brother Nature Produce located in Detroit on Rosa Park Boulevard for glorious greens and herbs.

My three little ones—Jacqueline, Natalie and Nico, all under 6 years old— keep the days and nights busy until, on Mother's Day, in May, we realize it's time to launch. Tasting and Touring Michigan begins!

First stop is Mesick, just west of Cadillac. In Grand Rapids, we pile into the minivan and head for the renowned Mesick Mushroom Festival. Our captain on this cruise, my husband, Rich, smacks his lips at the thought of tasty dishes I will whip up from our harvest of morel mushrooms. About 110 miles later, volunteers at the festival headquarters equip us with a picker's kit —including map and mesh bag—and we are introduced to the mushroom man himself. Carl Robinson, just shy of 90 at the time, escorts me in his all-wheel-drive truck.

Rich and the kids follow in the minivan. We pass the busy M-37/M-55 intersection, where entrepreneurs in pickups sell freshly harvested morels for many dollars a pound. Turning now, we rumble down a two-track into woods around Manistee National Forest.

"I've been hunting mushrooms since I was four," Carl says. "When we lived in Indiana, we had a farm with apple trees. Mushrooms grow better around fruit trees than anything else." Carl, who has run the Mesick festival since 1977, thinks the world of morels. "You can't beat the taste. (But) you got to clean them good; soak them overnight in salt water. Cut them in half and fry them in butter."

We bump down the gravel road into thick forest, park the vehicles, and hunt.

"A lot of mushrooms grow around ash trees."

"A lot of mushrooms grow around ash trees," Carl says. "You have got to have rain and heat; they like the moisture."

The overall you-pick seasons along Lake Michigan's fruit belt start in early to mid-June and run for months, until apples and pears are picked into October. While mass-produced, mass-market foods seem to dull the senses with their lack of connection to the earth, nothing reconnects you quite like a pick-your-own outing to stock the freezer.

Green spikes of flavor

In the West Michigan near-shore growing environment, particularly from Ottawa and Kent counties north to Oceana County, asparagus is the

Soon enough, we spy a fat, golden morel and jump for joy. "Knock things out of your way," directs Carl, who steadies himself with a cane his father once used. We snoop around for more, but not much luck. We painstakingly forage the forest, and Carl keeps encouraging us, but the harvest is thin today. Still, it's a great experience, and one you can only do "in season," of course.

Naturally, most small-scale farmers enthusiastically encourage people to eat in-season foods as they ripen regionally: "We find we have more celebration and joy when we eat in-season," explains Michael VanderBrug, co-owner of the Trillium Haven farm with his wife, Anja Mast, in Jenison. "Our kids will eat just gallons of strawberries for a couple of weeks, and then (the berries) are gone. By the time they are gone, you have had your fill, and you wait a year and gorge yourself again."

first king of spring. Sure, supermarkets bring in transcontinental asparagus as early as Easter, and sometimes year-round. The fresh local spears, though, are amazing edibles truly worth the wait for the real Michigan thing.

"Nobody says, 'I waited all year for green beans.' Nobody says ooh and aah for any other vegetables but asparagus," says Julie Dillingham, who owns and operates the largest asparagus farm in the state with her husband, Steve.

"Asparagus is an unusual vegetable. We're still picking on a crown that went in 20 years ago. People are passionate about it and crazy for it. I've got customers who come every night for 20 (days). They eat all the fresh asparagus they can get in season."

During asparagus prime time of late May through mid-June, which coincides with the National Asparagus Festival in Oceana County, Julie Dillingham, along with her daughter, Michelle, who was crowned Mrs. Asparagus for 1994, and granddaughter, Malaina Monroe, run a roadside stand. Asparagus for sale, $1 a pound lately, on the honor system. Their sign: 'Self-serve. Put money in can. Thank you.' Julie takes pride in her produce. "I want to put out a product that is as good as they can get."

It's a never-ending job, though. In the "everything" shed, minutes after the asparagus is harvested, Julie and her family wash, trim and sort by hand. They package the spears in one-, two- and five-pound bundles, cinching the clear plastic bags in the middle to resemble a floral bouquet.

"My grandchildren and I picked 500 pounds this morning. As soon as I can, I get the field heat out of the asparagus. I get cold water right on it. When it's picked

daily, you can take it home and keep it for a week. I can easily go through 200 pounds of asparagus out here," says Julie, waving toward the road-side stand. "Let's see, we haven't quite hit 500 pounds today, but we will because this is Asparagus Festival weekend."

Julie and Steve started in the 1960s with three acres; now they work 500. Steve says, "I've got a ledger I started in 1969. Julie and I walk-picked and got one pail of asparagus—12 pounds. In 2008, we harvested 1.6 million pounds." The bulk of it, he says, goes to the regional frozen packager Arbor Farms, also in Oceana County.

Only a few states, California and Michigan among them, harvest a sizable asparagus crop, because it is a costly, labor-intensive crop. And when it's ready, it's really ready. A healthy spear can grow four to six inches overnight.

"Asparagus is an unusual vegetable."

Like many perennial foods, new asparagus plants need a year or two of root development before their tempting shoots can be harvested. Once established, a crown of shoots can be quite the producer. In the field, seasonal-harvest workers ride mechanized picker contraptions designed by Steve. They sit low to the ground and snap off stalks as they roll by. It looks like the workers are dealing a deck of cards.

Steve says he is careful to keep a healthy balance on his land. "See, this field has weeds in it because it is

blanket, making the soil nutrient-dense. It's the most beautiful feeling when we're done picking and we seed this rye right away," Steve says while munching on an asparagus stalk in the field, Julie and Malaina nearby.

"The asparagus starts to come up, and it's just green like a lawn. It is a warm and fuzzy feeling that's so natural instead of barren from all the chemicals. We have virtually removed 99 percent of the herbicides out of our fields, so you can go in and plant anything, and there is no carry-over."

First round of berries

Sometimes the stars align and asparagus picking overlaps with strawberries ripening. No matter what the calendar shows, nothing says "Summer's here!" better than that. Suanne Dunneback Shoemaker, from a family farm north of Grand Rapids, grows strawberries, and she picks them at succulent ripeness, not just on a timetable from a supermarket buyer. The Dunneback berries are red through-and-through; no tough white cores here.

Suanne is on a first-name basis with her plants, calling them Jewels, Allstars, Earliglows, Darsalect, Honeye. "Some of them have beautiful names," she says.

How to choose between all those varieties? It depends on your plans for the fruit. When making jam, go for darker red Jewels for a luscious preserved taste. The

healthy enough for weeds to grow. We want to keep the weeds down, not obliterate everything."

Natural weed control

After the asparagus harvest, Dillingham "over-seeds" the fields with rye, a fast-growing cover crop that helps control weeds naturally. Working with Michigan State University "Green Grant" scientist Dan Brainard and his colleagues, Steve is able to farm without applying any herbicides. The rye gives off natural toxins to weeds. We've been using rye for a cover crop since the late '80s. The rye, under the ground, is like a nitrogen

lighter orangey-red All-Star variety ripens toward the end of season and freezes well. Early arrivers Honeye and French Darsalect yield large-scale sweetness that's yummy for snacking, freezing, and baking. Earliglows and Everbearing are versatile, hardy types home gardeners might want to try.

How to handle strawberries? If they're headed for the freezer, do not wash them. You can push the hulls out with a plastic drinking straw by poking the straw through the pointy end and up through the leafy green stem. On a cookie sheet, place the unwashed berries in a single layer. When frozen to full hardness, place them in zip-locking freezer bags. And when it's time to use some, quickly rinse the berries while frozen and get to work on the recipe: pie, cobbler, coffeecake, squares, oatmeal, jam... it's all good.

Having known Suanne since before "married with

> "I'm up at 5 a.m. and we're picking strawberries at 6:30 a.m."

Eight miles wide and 20 miles long, the prime fruit-growing ridge boasts near-perfect growing conditions—including loamy-to-clay soil and warming air and moisture from Lake Michigan to the west. In this agricultural sweet spot, Suanne grows her acreage of strawberries on two fields.

To keep the family enterprise going, Suanne opened a farm store filled with lovely things: canning supplies, aprons, table linens, tableware, jams, seasonal fruits and vegetables from The Ridge. There's even a bakery churning out fresh pies and doughnuts.

"We're always adding different things, trying to figure out what

children," I always have fun catching up with her about things. Over several recent summers, when I would show up with another baby in tow, Suanne got the biggest kick out of my brood. One year, I didn't quite make it to the last day of berry picking, but Shoemaker was certain I was coming and had reserved for me three flats of lovely berries for my gift-giving jars of jam. Yes, a relationship with local farmers is the real thing.

While it all sounds wonderful, Suanne always cautions that farming is an incredible gamble with the vagaries of Mother Nature. One recent year, when a late-spring freezing drizzle gripped blossoming plants in glittering ice, Shoemaker and her family rushed to the fields to run a $25,000 emergency "frost fan" unit. Then, record rainfall that June flash-plumped the berries with moisture, leading to a threat of deadly mold on the plants.

"It's challenging to grow nice, plump strawberries," says Suanne, whose farm is located on the climatologically favorable "Fruit Ridge," an elevated topographical terrain in West Michigan that drinks in Lake Michigan's breezes for a fine place to grow fruit.

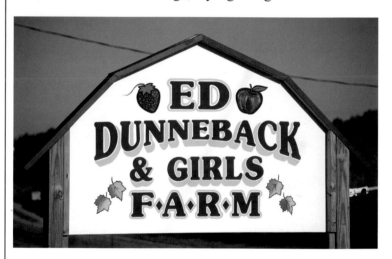

works," says Suanne, a member of North American Farmers' Direct Marketing Association, which shares marketing strategies among its members. Suanne's latest marketing strategy is on display: Cookie sheets filled with apple cinnamon and blueberry doughnuts cooling until they can be frosted. Mmmmm.

A bit-of-everything farm

Nearly a century of stories can be told by the Dunneback family—especially about the barn, where the store now operates. Back in the day, Shoemaker's grandfather used to have wedding receptions and parties in there. The farm goes way back, but things nearly didn't work out. In 1969, Ed Dunneback's boy, his only son, died in Vietnam. The loss was devastating.

"Michael went in December and was killed in March," Suanne said. "It was a hard time for us."

One day, though, Pam Dunneback May took a hard look at the Ed Dunneback & Son sign still painted on the barn. Pam leaned a big ladder up on the wall, climbed right up and painted the word "Girls" right over "Son." Today, Suanne and her daughters, Sarah Stoddard and Stephanie Shoemaker, run the place. Suanne is bent on keeping her small family farm solvent. She puts up Bing sweet cherries for sale, plus tart cherries, many apple varieties, pumpkins from carving types to pie types, tomatoes, and corn. An entertaining corn maze also operates each fall, and a cousin of Suanne's grazes a few dozen Black Angus cows that people like to come out and see.

Suanne waves to every farm-type truck running by on Six Mile Road. "We're trying to do whatever I can handle down here," said Suanne, who joined the American Agri-Women organization, looking for sisterhood. American Agri-Women, representing tens of thousands of women involved in agriculture, established a trademark program, American Grown Goodness, as

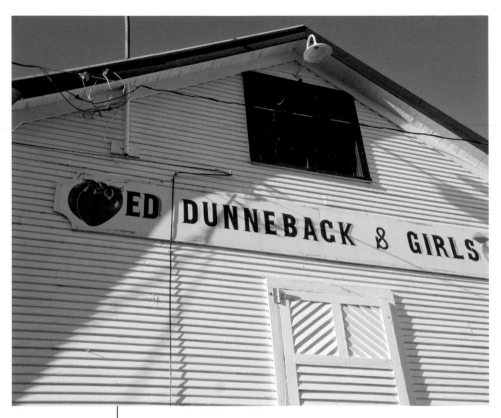

a way for growers, processors and marketers to identify their American-grown products for the consumer.

All things berry and Berry

As more people demand produce grown in ecologically sound ways and closer to home, organic blueberry growers John Van Voorhees and Joan Donaldson are way ahead of the curve, having worked this way for 30 years.

During the back-to-the-land movement of the 1970s and '80s, the married couple made a home for themselves in a peat-bog tract in Allegan County. In a simple farmhouse heated by a wood-burning cookstove, they started living close to the land—and far from the romanticized way city dwellers sometimes imagine.

Joan Donaldson vividly recalls those early years: "We read (renowned farmer-philosopher) Wendell Berry's *The Unsettling of America: Culture and Agriculture,* when it came out in the late '70s and started to think about the future of our whole culture, character and agriculture. At times, when it was rough—and those years when things were dying of drought—we would stop and think about what he said. So when I met him, this wonderful poet-farmer, I said, 'You changed my life.' He said, 'I hope that I made it better.'"

"Ask yourself this: Where is your place?"

Joan says she replied, "You did." After nearly memorizing that author's critical yet optimistic assessment of the American family farm, Joan says, she realized America's wholesale disconnect from the land added to a host of modern-day problems.

"Ask yourself this: Where is your place? How can you make your place (in the world)? Nurture the land that sustains and grounds you."

It's postcard-pretty down a long dirt drive to their gardening shed. Nearby, the couple's American Gothic two-story home, still partially under construction, serves as the headquarters of Pleasant Hill Farm, the organic blueberry operation thriving in their nicely moist, peat-laden soil.

Varieties grown here include Bluecrop, Jersey, Elliott, Duke, Rubel, and Bluejay. "There are many different varieties of blueberries, just like apples, but it's harder to tell them apart," John says. "It's easier to tell the difference between a Gala and Honeycrisp (apple)."

The farming partners, both graduates of Hope College, in nearby Holland, are looking to expand their lineup into peaches, strawberries, and raspberries. "Over and over, people are asking us for it," Joan says. "We already have the market."

They've been doing organic for a long time, even before the Community Supported Agriculture (CSA) movement in the mid-1980s attracted urban consumers to the idea of fresh, eco-friendly produce, dairy, and meat from nearby farms.

"We were part of the back-to-the-landers in the '70s," Joan says. "Most people eventually went back to the cities. A few stayed, and we were one of the families that toughed it out. We've had good years and bad years, just like any farmer. Lately we had some wet years; so wet you can't get down there to mow or spray because of all the rain."

Thirty years ago, from their rural Fennville fields, things didn't go so well when they first sold produce at a nearby farmers market. Few were willing to spend the extra pennies on organic blueberries back then; it seemed the only driving factor for consumers was lowest price. The market has slowly changed, though. "We've done a lot of education, about growing in a way that is good and safe for us and the land," John says. Originally certified by Organic Growers of Michigan, Pleasant Hill blueberries now carry the internationally recognized Oregon Tilth Certified Organic (OTCO) label. Because of the soil's high organic content

and the years of sustainable farming, the blueberries are extra sweet and intensely flavorful.

Some of the berry bushes here were planted in the 1940s by John's grandfather and uncles. "Grandpa bought the farm in 1937. I am a third-generation blueberry farmer," John explains as he rushes a shipment for Cherry Capital Foods, an independent, statewide distributor they use. "If my son came back (into the business) he would be fourth; but I don't think he's coming."

The couple started with six acres and slowly expanded to 40. Early in the season, Pleasant Hill hosts a short you-pick operation before there are enough blueberries to shake off the bushes for bulk sale. Because the farm doesn't hire seasonal workers, John says, the crop after you-pick goes to organic-foods market. "We shake off the blueberries with a machine. If people want fresh, they have to come out and pick."

Thinking outside the (blueberry) box, John and Joan created an online business model to help the bottom line. During the harvest, they freeze 10- and 35-pound boxes of their organic product and, through the winter, insulated containers packed with dry ice are available for purchase. They ship on Tuesdays so the frozen order arrives before the weekend.

"It's like a renaissance," says Joan, who is a renaissance woman herself, with a master's degree in writing from Spalding University in Louisville, Kentucky. The children's book author also writes personal essays about farm and home life, appearing over the years in *The Christian Science Monitor, Ideals Magazine, Rosebud Magazine*, and several anthologies. It's interesting how things change, Joan says, explaining that Pleasant Hill today is competing against other or-

ganic blueberries—but they are raised and shipped from Chile and Argentina, which flies in the face of local-food thinking. "If you buy a (plastic) clamshell of organic blueberries, check the label; they probably came from South America," Joan says.

Join the farmer through a CSA

Eater's Guild Farm, operated as a Community Supported Agriculture outlet, rambles along a county road outside of Bangor, in the southwestern corner of the state. Overgrown landscape nearly obscures the brick Victorian house and signage. About a dozen muddy, tall rubber boots—Wellies, they're called—lean into one another, clustering around the kitchen door. Farm buildings, some studies in crumbling charm, contain great clumps of harvested garlic hanging from the rafters to dry. Others hold bales of hay and a stable of Nubian and Alpine goats.

Chickens of the Freedom Ranger variety, slow-growing birds developed a half-century ago in France, scratch and peck and scurry just the way chickens are supposed to—free in the barnyard, getting fresh air. Freedom Ranger is a favorite meat chicken on many small farms. Lee Arboreal, who owns the farm with his wife, Laurie, loves the variety. "They're good broilers. We originally had 100, but we're probably down to 70 of them because of some foxes playing with the farm lately," he says. The couple met up north when he worked at an apple

orchard in Frankfort and she managed a food co-op in Mount Pleasant. Then they purchased this organic farm, which they saw advertised in the *Michigan Organic Farm Alliance* publication. Quaint and still rustic by most modern tastes, Lee and Laurie brought the farm back to life. "It looked so overrun, like a Mayan temple," Lee recalls.

Tapping into his internship at an organic CSA in Oregon, Lee quickly had Eater's Guild up and running after they closed on the property. A CSA is an agreement between a farmer and individual to share the bounty and risks of the growing season. Increasingly, the contracts are helping small-scale family farms remain viable by opening a totally local market for their goods. No middleman for marketing

"Farming affects you like a disease, more than anything. You can't stop thinking about it."

and mark-up. No long-distance transport of the produce. No daunting supermarket agreements. However, because a farmer is just one bad storm, freeze, drought, or freak accident away from a losing season, a CSA is no miracle solution. It can help, though. In 2001, Lee and Laurie started their CSA with 25 families. Ten years after, Eater's Guild sells out its annual shares and has a waiting list for membership. Lee, who has a bachelor's degree in religion from Central Michigan University, says the CSA system means everything to them. "It was really one of the only ways to start a young farm," he says.

"Farming affects you like a disease, more than anything. You can't stop thinking about it. It's a good way to use different parts of your body, to access all your resources. There's all kinds of problem-solving you got to do. The work makes you feel whole. You don't need exercise at a gym because farmwork makes you sleep well."

Pay your part

At the beginning of the season, shareholders pay $285 to $500, depending on share type, for the season. That gets you 25 weeks of produce in this growing climate, including as many as 40 kinds of produce for the table. Depending on the CSA system employed, shareholders may be able to come out and work the land, but they don't have to at Eater's Guild; it's not required. Sound like a fresh, tasty idea? It is, but it's not all sweetness and light. It's a lot of work.

Lee, Laurie, their daughter, Iris, and baby son, Leif, don't have time for things like TV. They have to give themselves completely to the life. Laurie is knee-deep in the tough stuff, too: "I am forever trying to squash the stereotype that the man does the farming and the woman doesn't," says Laurie, who earned her bachelor's in zoology from Louisiana State University.

"I, too, am in the field, making deliveries, and selling to stores and farmers market. Most often, the whole family does it (together)."

Lee and Laurie sell fine organic produce to their shareholders and at farmers markets in Holland, South Haven, and Texas Township. A few local restaurants also buy from them.

On a Tuesday—CSA delivery day—things are bustling at Eater's Guild as member boxes are filled. At the barn, five young hired hands (fresh-faced college

students or recent grads) prep clumps of German "porcelain hardneck" garlic for distribution. The variety is extra hardy for cold climates.

Looking to make the farm more profitable, the Arboreals are experimenting with raising turkeys, plus a duck flock for eggs, which should fetch a better return on investment than their chicken broilers, Laurie says. They are building a goat herd, too, primarily Nubian and Alpine, and a small investment in cows. The couple would love to struggle less and live more, they say, so they're creating some value-added products such as cured meats and handcrafted cheese. "We're after a little less bending over to harvest," Lee says. "We want to stand up to do our work, as our backs get older. And less annual and more perennial crop."

In the rambling brick Victorian house, Laurie, with 9-month-old Leif on her hip, warms big pots of raw, non homogenized goat milk to make cheese. "Last year, we stored nearly 60 pounds of cheese," she says while leafing through her papers on cheese-making. Sometimes, Lee and Laurie just have to slow down and catch their breath, they say. "This was a resting year," Lee explains. "We had a baby last winter, so we've pared it down to basics, and we're hitting those hard, like potatoes, carrots, onions, garlic, cooking greens (kale, collards, chard)—the things we use most every day. We're letting the farm evolve a bit (because) we can't be doing this annual stuff for the rest of our lives."

On delivery day, Lee is on the road by 3:30 p.m. to drop off member boxes in the parking lot of a Kalamazoo chiropractic office. Just a road-trip break, though, because when he's back home, it's out to the field to harvest for two farmers markets and a store they help supply.

Matt Steele, an intern for Lee and Laurie who finished at Michigan State University recently with a degree in food safety and processing, sees good things at Eater's Guild. "There's a passion here. This is a different lifestyle, being out here. I grew up about the farthest away from a farm as you get—in the suburbs."

Fall into this food

Michigan in early October is an incredibly welcoming time and place, with cornflower-blue skies, crisp air, and the land heavy with harvest-ready foods.

At Trillium Haven, the farm in Jenison, winter squash is piled high in huge wooden crates offering up acorn, butternut, buttercup, and many other varieties.

Two black kettles percolate apple cider on an open flame this fall day as a special occasion is at hand, with a harvest feast and panel discussion on tap. Paper lanterns light the way to the open seating, where a pole-barn outbuilding offers guests a buffet of butternut squash with aromatic Indian seasoning, collard greens, sausage and bean soup, and a Southeast Asian noodle soup. It's shot through with the warm flavors of autumn. Kids carve pumpkins nearby while dozens of grown-ups linger over the harvest spread. It's gorgeous here at Trillium Haven, especially given that the whole affair is homegrown and handcrafted by friends and neighbors.

This event, The Future For Food discussion, sponsored by Rapid Growth Media, features local culinary experts who are trying to change the food landscape in West Michigan and beyond. Trillium Haven hosts a number of events, inviting city folk each year to

a spring open house, a tomato canning festival, heirloom tomato tasting, potato festival, fall events with pumpkin carving and wagon rides, and cooking classes year-round with popular chef Amy Sherman.

The farm owners, Anja Mast and her husband, Michael VanderBrug, say it's all worth the effort. "There are so many things people want to know, and that is, in and of itself, a whole bunch of good."

When the two Calvin College graduates converted Michael's grandfather's farm to a CSA operation, it was clear a bit of "educating the public" needed to happen. The couple wanted the CSA concept to catch on, and so Trillium Haven began, on only a couple of acres.

Today, shareholders at Trillium Haven get a guaranteed percentage of the harvest, from $545 to $565 per season, with $100 off for four hours of weekly farm work. That membership yields 22 weeks of produce, including 47 kinds of vegetables in 400 total varieties. Anja is a bit of a darling of the Grand Rapids food scene these days. She's everywhere, talking about cooking from scratch with whole foods, buying from local farms, eating in season, and teaching our taste buds the difference between sub-par fare and downright delicious. After Mast's CSA operation was going well, Trillium Haven partnered in 2007 with local garden-plant supplier Luurtsma Distribution to start a certified organic plant/herb line, "Harvest in Harmony," which is distributed in garden centers throughout the Midwest.

From the field to the people

Anja and Michael are thankful for the Fulton Street Farmers Market in Grand Rapids. Every week, Trillium Haven ferries a truckload to the city market and sells from a three-stall space. It's an outlet for their product that can't be beat, and a great source for new CSA members. "The first 10 years of our farm has been 80 percent education" wherever potential customers gather, Michael says. Anja goes to churches, schools, and community groups with cooking demonstrations and more. "We know the (local) food movement isn't moving ahead without people learning how to cook. Raw food is scary to lots of people, especially when it has all the leaves, stems and roots attached. That is what we're up against."

Anja says it shouldn't be that scary. "Why do we like grandma's food? Because she went out to her garden, picked some food, and made it on the spot. Perhaps she made the most gorgeous bread, or homemade ice cream. That is stuff we have forgotten." Anja says she would like to see the day when people value healthy, hearty food the way they value their smart phones and big TVs. "Talk to me when three percent of the food produced in the state is consumed in the state, because we're not even at one percent. Farming is the hardest work you will ever do. We know so many good, good farmers who love what they do and care about their land and community, but who can't compete against cheaper food grown elsewhere.

"If farmers can't make a living from what they do, then we just won't have this younger generation take over

their family's farms. It's frustrating to see people settle for bland, unprocessed food, which actually ends up costing more than what they can make for themselves at home," Anja says. "We've forgotten what good food tastes like, but our taste buds can be woken up—like when you take a bite of a fresh, just-picked Michigan peach in the summer, or when you pick basil from your own garden and learn to whip up a simple pesto pasta dish."

City's gone country

Discovery and delight can greet a culinary road-tripper on any Michigan road. Many Detroiters, for example, are beginning to see urban agriculture as a real part of the solution; to grow things right where people live, where they work, and definitely need healthier food on the table. Green city gardens are scattered throughout Detroit now, from the schoolyard at Catherine Ferguson Academy for pregnant teens and teen moms, to re-claimed land owned by a local order of Catholic friars (Earthworks), to a seven-acre organic farm in Rouge Park. Together, city gardeners, nonprofit organizations, and the Greening of Detroit resource agency are writing a new local-food story of urban Michigan. Take Brother Nature for example. Scarlett runner beans robustly frame the greenhouse door on a city lot along Rosa

Parks Boulevard, and this is where Greg Willerer, a.k.a. Brother Nature, plucks a pretty red blossom that he says is edible and quite tasty at that. "The (blossoms) grow a bean that is edible. Take the little green part, hold it and bite off the red part. They taste like a bean." Greg takes us on a taste tour of the place, which is Detroit's first CSA farm, a one-acre enterprise bordered by chain-link fences, sidewalks, and city streets. Here, Brother Nature works greenhouses and rows of organic-soil garden enriched by compost from the nearby Motor City Brewing Works. Greg grows in raised beds, as many urban gardeners must, because of concern that the soil might be contaminated with lead-paint chips or the rubble of old construction.

He focuses on growing herbs, salad greens, and heirloom tomatoes.

On this hot summer day, Greg, who was a social studies teacher in Chicago and Detroit for 15 years, is getting ready for his member visits. It is the CSA's distribution day, and each shareholder gets a cardboard box full of herbs, greens, heirloom tomatoes, vegetables, house-made hot sauce, and a bunch of flowers. Greg hopes to double his acreage soon, and he just planted 80 heirloom raspberry bushes and 100 strawberries. All the while, he tries to have fun, too. Greg recently hosted Detroit's first chicken race, with a roster of 15 birds. "They didn't race," he laments. "They came out and scratched. But 200 people came out to see it (and) celebrate what we're trying to start here.

Greg grows some very special varieties. There are black cherry tomatoes, which are maroon-colored little flavor bombs, and six varieties of mizuma, a Japanese green from the mustard family with a taste that's hot, like arugula. Also purslane. "Have you ever tried purslane? It is wonderful, especially when mixed with things like lemon basil. This is golden purslane, which is a brother, or cousin, to purslane..Let me give you a taste of a couple of things. Lemon basil…you can smell it or eat it."

"opportunity to experiment"

Greg also qualifies as a kind of urban home-steader. His two-story Victorian home was built from a 1915 Sears kit. "This was a big mess," Greg says of the area.

A neighborhood "wild" cat named Trillium ambles by, and Greg mentions that he's trying to keep Trillium around for pest management. He says a family of pheasants also pecks around in bushes on the edge of his property.

"We call Detroit the urban prairie." Others in the city collaborate with Greg. Kate Devlin, from Spirit Farms, has reclaimed three vacant lots and provides vegetables, salad greens, and herbs for his Brother Nature Produce CSA. He also sells to eight independently owned restaurants and at two farmers markets, one at Wayne State University and the other, the big Eastern Market.

For under used urban spaces, there are some grand ideas out there. On parcels of open land within depopulated sections of Detroit, for example, some groups are seeking to introduce large-scale conventional farming, but there are several obstacles to that idea, the largest one being mass moves to gather widely dispersed Detroiters into compact neighborhoods. Doing so would open up large tracts for tractor farming.

"One of things I just love about doing (a farm in the city) is the opportunity to experiment," Greg said. "I don't want to grow the three or four things people always reach for. I like the almost improvisational stuff, to experiment. To come up with new combinations."

At the Wayne State farmers market, Greg whips up and sells organic salads-to-go with heirloom tomatoes, edible flowers and from-scratch dressing made by the local Mudgie's Deli. For just four bucks!

Farming in D-Town

The first time Ebony Roberts tried a ground cherry was a big surprise in a little package. Ebony peeled away the papery husk, like a tomatillo's, and found a teeny, cherry-size fruit inside. "They are one of the most delicious things in the world. When you pop them up in your mouth, they taste golden."

Ebony farms a bit of land on the western edge of Detroit. Along with Malik Yakini and a handful of African American activists, Ebony helped launch D-Town Farm, which is short for Detroit Black Community Food Security Farm. In the Rouge Park neighborhood, they bring locally grown, nutrient-dense foods to city dwellers. Deeply concerned about health and nutrition issues, D-Town Farm promotes urban farming, food co-ops, youth training programs, cooking classes, and more.

"We really wanted to reintroduce our people to our agriculture heritage," says Ebony as we chat in a Royal Oak coffeehouse before hitting the local farmers market.

"We're just a generation or two from the family farm. My grandmother always had a garden in her backyard. She is 85 and just stopped gardening a few years ago because she couldn't get down and do it herself. So much intuitive knowledge hasn't been passed down and is in danger of being lost altogether. People knew when to plant because they looked in the almanac; they knew when the sun and moon were in the certain positions, when the earth had warmed up enough to put the seed in the ground.

"We're highlighting this legacy," she says. "We want to pass on this knowledge."

Ebony says many younger city dwellers, those under 40 or so, negatively equate farming somehow with slavery and/or sharecropping.

"In reality, urban farming gives you the resources to feed your family healthier choices. You are getting control of your food system in your family. Now that's power."

In many core cities, she says, fresh produce is almost unavailable while processed, high-calorie junk food and sugary beverages abound.

D-Town Farm started operating on a small tract of donated land. Eventually, in 2008, the organic urban farm carved out two acres in Rouge Park, at a former tree nursery, and signed a 10-year lease with the city. The group favored what is informally called "lasagna gardening," a no-till, no-dig method that calls for layering organic matter to stack up and grow things slightly above grade.

D-Towners created structure-free, raised beds and put down layers of earth-friendly burlap, newsprint, compost, and soil. They soon discovered the lasagna method retains water very well, discourages weeds and creates easy-to-work soil. Soon, D-Town volunteers also built two hoop-houses, which

are essentially cold-frame structures placed over the garden soil. The group also is putting five more acres into cultivation, which will be a big leap in capacity.

Many D-Town members are active in Greening of Detroit, an agriculture resource agency dedicated to reclaiming neglected urban acreage and growing good food in the city. Grown in Detroit, a farm-to-market offshoot of Greening of Detroit, helps set up small growers at the huge Eastern Market. The growers simply hand over their goods to Grown in Detroit, which then sells them at Eastern Market through rotating booth volunteers from among the growers. Everyone pitches in at some point, and then the proceeds are distributed accordingly. Grown in Detroit also does the paperwork and pays the booth and insurance fees, leaving the growers to concentrate on their produce and customers.

D-Town Farm also participates in Wayne State University Farmers Market, Northwest Detroit Farmers Market, and the Joy Southfield Farmers Market.

D-Town's strategic plan for the next several years calls for planting fruit and nut trees, creating value-added products, introducing chickens to the farm for eggs and fertilizer, expanding its mushroom business to include shiitake, morel, and chanterelles, and keeping bees to market honey. Also under discussion is starting a mobile food truck, similar to a bookmobile, to bring fresh produce to those who can't get to the market. Considering that some families' only access to food is whatever the nearby liquor store stocks, this could be a big deal, indeed.

The non-profit received a $149,940 grant from the Kellogg Foundation to strengthen the network of African American urban farmers in inner-city Detroit, and D-Town farmers are improving the urban soil in open lots citywide.

"There is so much to learn," Ebony says of the whole discipline of farming in the big city. "It is absolutely fascinating."

HomeGrown party time

The Scene: Ann Arbor HomeGrown Festival on a late-September Saturday at the Ann Arbor Farmers Market.

The Dilemma: How to choose from so many tantalizing heirloom tomatoes in striking shades and stripes of yellow, orange, purple, even chocolate.

Old-fashioned veggie strains, called heirlooms, come in all shapes, sizes, and colors but lost favor in the modern, mass-marketplace because they don't ship and keep as well as the typical tomato hybrid.

At the HomeGrown Festival, Project Grow Community Gardens' tomato tasting event features a dazzling collection of heirlooms. Volunteers slice and dice dozens of kinds, serving them by toothpick, like canapés. On offer are Principe Borghese, an Italian heirloom that is a favorite for drying; a striped Green Zebra; an Italian Costoluto Genovese with pretty little flutes and pleats, and a West Virginia Hillbilly orange-yellow variety.

Marcell Tractman offers the fresh-cut goodies to a throng of foodies. "You're welcome to try as many as you like," she says. There's bold Brandywine, the quintessential heirloom because of its multipurpose qualities in the kitchen. Next, fetchingly named tomatoes draw tasters. They try superstar Black Zebra, peachy-colored Garden Peach, ivory-colored Snow White, and an orange-hued beefsteak Jimbo from Kentucky.

Marcell says the heirlooms are grown organically from seed in the nonprofit Project Grow gardens. "It (is) continuing a link to past generations and maintaining genetic diversity in our foods," she says of sustaining the old varieties. Project Grow's tasting event, meanwhile, tries to spark interest in growing heirlooms in backyards and community gardens, and to introduce to people the hundreds of varieties still out there. To help the tomato gene pool, Project Grow saves, grows, and sells seedlings at the People's Food Co-op in Ann Arbor, across from the city-run Farmers Market.

"Heirlooms aren't just old-fashioned stuff but are really tasty tomatoes."

"Heirlooms aren't just old-fashioned stuff but are really tasty tomatoes. They were grown organically at the beginning, because that's what all farmers did before World War II," Marcell says. "They are absolutely suited to organic gardening."

The 40-year-old Project Grow also manages community garden sites with hundreds of plots tended by the public. At its Discovery Gardens, located at the Leslie Science & Nature Center and County Farm Park, Project Grow runs programming for kids, seniors and gardeners with disabilities. The group registers Ann Arbor residents every year for plots, and "We always fill up," Marcell says.

berries, herbs, flowers, plants, and roots, for her hand-blended, fair-trade-certified teas. Her temple of all things tea, built from lumber cut from her land, sits on 12 acres she cultivates for her Light of Day Organics product line. In this oasis of calm is found an amazing diversity of plants. There are blueberries named Jersey and Blueray, strawberries both ever-bearing and June-bearing, raspberries and elderberries to flavor the tea blends, beets and Roma tomatoes for vegetable teas; and asters, buttercups, chrysanthemums, and towering sunflowers, some growing just for the local bees, birds, and butterflies.

"I plant 10 percent extra for nature," Angela says. "Twenty percent of my 25 acres is left alone so it's protected space for the animals." Besides the planting on this large parcel, she grows 12 acres at her home, just a mile down the road.

Angela, a former open-heart and ER registered nurse, became a horticulturist to create fair-trade tea that was pure, wholesome, and good for the body and soul. She micromanages every step to ensure product quality, including tilling the soil, planting the heirloom seeds she collects, hand harvesting the crops and then drying, blending and packaging the teas with great care. She ships the products to independently owned restaurants and stores.

Traversing north for tea

About eight miles west of Traverse City, Angela Macke is determined to grow a local tea industry. Farming organically, Angela grows 240 items, including

It all started when Angela was diagnosed with Crohn's disease and lupus, two very challenging auto-immune conditions. She left her nursing career in the ER behind. "I knew I needed (my own) 911; I needed emergency aid to my immune system," Angela says of her move to blend her own teas.

"When I started to make my teas with organic ingredients that I bought from the store, I would taste this creepy aftertaste. I was, like, 'What is that?'" So she sent the store-bought organic ingredients to have them tested at university labs, which found pesticide residue all over them, she says. Then and there, she decided to blend her own product. Seven years ago, she starting gifting her new tea blends for Christmas and her company soon was launched.

"This has become my gift, my passion," Angela says. "It's the only way I could keep doing all of this. The tea leaf is the most labor-intensive crop known to man; tea plants (bushes) can grow up to 40 feet. And on the plantation, it takes 70,000 leaves (and lots of hand labor) for one pound of finished product. That is why fair-trade certification is so important. We wanted to make sure that taste wasn't the only thing to feel good about."

Light of Day sells more than 40 loose-leaf teas, mainly black, green, and oolong, plus blends, herbal infusions, scented varieties and more. Packaged in gift-worthy polished silver tins, the teas elegantly line one wall. One example, cherry mint tea, is blended with organic white tea, Montmorency cherries, hibiscus, spearmint, peppermint and maple syrup bits. Take the

time to smell the heartwarming cinnamon tea blended with rooibos, apple, orange, clove and cinnamon.

On our visit to Light of Day, a large carafe offers hummingbird nectar, the flavor of the day. It is a blend of cherry, hibiscus, blueberry, grape, currant, elderberry and more. You feel like a hummingbird feeding on nectar.

With afternoon light shining a halo on the tea store, Angela and two employees prepare for a tea cupping, $15 per person. Similar to a wine tasting, a tea cupping invites you to sample various brewed teas and tea-infused dishes. To appreciate the teas, Angela suggest skipping coffee that day, brushing your teeth prior to the event, and tasting each type straight, without milk or sugar. Scrutinize the tea before sipping, she says. Then sip and roll it on the tongue.

"With tea, you start with the sort of light, white teas or the less flavorful ones and work your way up. When you go to a cupping, think about your palate. Think about the things that can effect your palate and stay away from peppery, spicy foods, garlic for sure, anything that might linger."

A super-antioxidant tea smoothie concludes the tasting. Angela whirls in a blender Matcha tea powder with Rice Dream frozen rice milk. She passes out samples of the fine green

Matcha powder, almost a dust. "It is stone-ground 50 percent finer than talcum powder." Matcha contains more antioxidants per serving than any other product in the world, she says.

"This has become my gift, my passion."

It's a grind; that's good

Westwind Milling's motto, "We grow it, we mill it, we bake it," implies how very fresh everything is here. Westwind Milling, a certified organic stone mill in the Genesee County town of Linden, sells high-quality small-batch flours crafted from its own grain fields and those of 16 other organic Michigan farms. Lee and Linda Purdy grow their wheat without synthetic fertilizers or pesticides, in soil that has been enriched with fresh manures and compost. They plant hard red spring wheat called Dakota (a high-gluten grain planted in the spring and harvested in August), plus hard red winter wheat, soft winter white, and durum. They also grow buckwheat, rye, corn, and more.

Grain brought in on a given morning is milled into flour and baked into bread that day. The bagged Westwind products—Wild Rose flour for bread, Sweet Pea for pastry, and others—look and feel different than the supermarket staples. Westwind turns out an excellent pesto bread made with basil and tomatoes from the property, and it is a meal all by itself.

The business operates from a mill structure dating to 1836, and grindstand, which does the heavy work, was created in the 1960s. The Purdys, husband and wife, are the first to tell you they had no business getting that mill, but if you believe in serendipity and happy endings, then this is a story for you.

"You know, there is a certain amount of desperation in all of the decisions that we make, and so

it starts out with a 160-acre farm that is a slow spiral, losing it just a little every year," Lee started out. "In the late '90s, early 2000s, we had the option of raising houses instead of grain. We could have sold off and made a lot of money in real estate, or we could be hard-headed and buy an old mill and try to make a market for our grain, which is what we did. If you don't believe in fate, you won't believe this story."

Argentine Township had been trying to rid itself of the mill and property (which it had purchased at $475,000), but there were no takers. Eventually, along came Lee and Linda, who snapped up the mill and three acres for $125,000. They figured it was meant to be and

started growing grains at their 120-acre farm about 12 miles north. They also diversified, growing grains that they milled and bagged, selling the small-batch flours as well as scone, cake, cornbread, muffins and pancake mixes —90 products in all—to farmers markets in Lansing and the Detroit area. Today, their products are sold in Ann Arbor, Dearborn, Ypsilanti, and on the Westwind Milling website.

Westwind Milling fits into the interesting category called medium millers, which do a mixed practice of wholesale and retail. The small mills only grind for their own use, while the larger millers, such as Star of the West in Frankenmuth, work for corporate clients such as Battle Creek's Kellogg and Chelsea's Jiffy, doing strictly wholesale.

Westwind's small-batch operation includes a bakery and mill store to educate people on the endless possibilities. The bakery turns out fresh organic breads and pastries on Tuesdays and Fridays during the winter, more often during the summer months. On weekends, tarts, scones, cookies, pies, and coffee cakes add to the bakery case.

The Purdys say they hope to expand even more, offering a gluten-free line, and building additional kitchens and a bake house. They want to provide a living wage for family members working at Westwind Milling and, to that end, they put in a licensed commercial kitchen to offer even more products in the years head.

A similar milling operation, Jennings Brothers Stone-Ground Grains, sells by e-mail at archiejennings63@gmail.com. Archie and Mattie Jennings will grind products fresh to your order and ship them to you. In the summer, Jennings Brothers can be found at the Fulton Street Farmers Market in Grand Rapids as well as at markets in Holland and Kalamazoo.

Beans in Howard City

Fran Arbogast-Carlson and her son, Brandon Carlson, are known to work 20-hour days when it's time to harvest the beans. But when it's not in the midst of harvest, it's great to chat a while with this hard-driving Michigan farm family. Arbogast-Carlson's three children got their degrees from Michigan State University—two in crop and soil science and one in agricultural engineering. They're all part of this farm's identity dating back to the 1840s.

"My great-grandparents grew beans in the 1800s," Fran says. "Their specialty was yellow-eyed beans, which we no longer grow." The yellow-eyes were big back then, she says, but now it's all about mayocoba beans. The oval-shaped, medium-size, ivory-yellow dry bean is popular in Latin American dishes and is similar to a pinto bean in appearance and flavor. It dresses up soups, salads and refried bean dishes.

"Latino people consider the pinto bean an everyday bean, the black bean is a Sunday bean, and the mayocoba is a celebration bean. They are so good. Wait until you try them," says Fran, who represents farmers as District 8 (West Michigan) commissioner for the Michigan Bean Commission. In her 13 years with the commission, she has traveled to Mexico, Spain, and France on bean-industry business.

Montcalm County grows several showy, colorful beans, including the sun-kissed, mayocoba, plus red kidney, Italian favorite cannelloni, cranberry, black, and pinto. The Saginaw Valley and Thumb area produces the vast majority of the state's dry bean crop, however, growing a greater quantity of workhouse beans such as pinto and navy. Their output secures Michigan's usual spot as a top dry-bean producer, usually competing with North Dakota and Nebraska in production. Michigan is the country's leading producer of black beans and the No. 2 producer of dry beans, an industry that added more than $100 million to the state's economy. If you've ever seen vine-like green beans growing in a garden, then you have a good idea of what dry beans look like. The vine-like plants, same species as green beans (snap beans,) reach anywhere from 18 to 24 inches tall, with pods running along the length of the stem.

They grow so good here," says Fran, who also served on the United States Bean Council for eight years and has worked bean promotions, recipe development, and much more over the years. "We have sandy soil (that beans) love because they don't like 'wet feet,' meaning, they don't like wet roots. If they get too wet, that actually stunts their growth. If we plant these beans in the spring and get a downpour, the beans don't do anything."

Fran is very pleased that son Brandon is taking on the family business. "I'm so lucky my son wants to farm." About 2,000 acres are under cultivation here, part of it rented to augment their own land.

"Many kids have no familiarity with beans."

"Many young people don't (stay in farming)," she says. "Look at the hours that he is working. We never know what we will get for our product, because we have all of these people above us, who will say, 'I will give you this or that for your product.' We don't ever know if we will make a profit."

On this visit to the bean farm, Brandon and farmhand, Eric, are running on harvest-time adrenaline as they run two pullers that rip the plants from the ground and place them in neat windrows for combining. "When it's time, we've got to be ready, because bad weather can stop the whole thing," Brandon says.

Carlson-Arbogast Farm rotates crops to replenish the soil, so every three years, beans are sidelined for corn and wheat, which are sent to King's Mill in Lowell.

Always the industry spokesperson, Fran wants to turn the tide by challenging families to cook a meal at home with Michigan beans. As a registered dietitian, Fran has cooked up tasty bean dishes in a demonstration project for children in the Greenville Public Schools. She introduced the youngsters to bean muffins, chicken noodle and bean soup, bean chili, and quesadillas, all of which have made an appearance on the school cafeteria's menu board.

"Many kids have no familiarity with beans," Fran said. "We need to educate them and their parents, because beans are a wonderful, high-quality protein at a low price. I don't know how beans got so downgraded as the poor man's food. The other day, I got so upset when I heard someone on the news saying the economy is so bad that 'We're back to eating beans.' I was aghast. Beans are one of the healthiest things you can eat … like a superfood full of health benefits."

That tangy red berry

On the shores of Lake Michigan, in Van Buren County, 40 acres of wetland bogs are used to grow cranberries, one of very few native North American fruit. These gorgeous big berries are nothing like those hard little maroon things at the supermarket. At DeGrandchamps Farm near South Haven, the Ben Lear variety of cranberry—one of six grown here—is a large fruit in a beautiful, blushing red. One of the few fruits you can't eat raw, the tart, tangy flavor of cranberries even comes through when thoroughly cooked with sugar.

"A lot of people don't know cranberries have varieties," says Mike DeGrandchamp. "They see the Early Blacks and Howes in the stores around Thanksgiving and think that's it." But it's not. Feast your eyes on the bright reds at DeGrandchamps; on the Stevens, Pilgrims, and more. On the large fruited gems that ripen in late September to early October.

In 1994, brothers Joe, Mike, and Bob DeGrandchamp decided to diversify their blueberry farm with a few test acres of cranberries. After their dad, the late Vincent DeGrandchamp, talked to a student from the now-defunct Western Michigan University Horticultural Economic Development Center about growing cranberries, the brothers decided to give it the old college try. They toured farms in Massachusetts and Wisconsin and built beds for the crop. Cranberries are among the most expensive crops to establish, costing as much as $50,000 an acre. Then, it takes three or four years for fruit to appear.

The DeGrandchamps harvested more than a half-million pounds of cranberries this year, making them the second-largest cranberry grower in Michigan. Sharon and Wally Huggett's farm in Cheboygan County has a larger stand of 150 acres of cranberries, which is about half of the state's total acreage. There are several small operations in the Upper Peninsula, including Centennial Cranberry Farm on the southern shore of Lake Superior, at Whitefish Point. Centennial has operated since 1876. All the other cranberry plantings in the state are in the five southern counties along Lake Michigan shore. Michigan's 307 acres aren't much against the 38,000 nationwide, of which 18,000 acres are in Wisconsin. But Michigan does possess the climatic conditions, acidic soils, and agricultural infrastructure needed to increase its cranberry production significantly.

At DeGrandchamps Farm, the berries are both dry- and wet-harvested. In the wet-harvest method, the bogs are flooded and the berries float to the surface to be collected by machine. "It's the only crop that I know of that is harvested by floating," Mike DeGrandchamps says. "The fruit is hollow inside; nothing weighs it down." Dry-harvest berries, picked by hand or machine, are destined for local markets in Kalamazoo, Grand Rapids, and Chicago, while 90 percent of the wet-harvest berries are processed into juice products.

Ed Dunneback & Girls Farm, 3025 Six Mile Road NW, Grand Rapids MI 49544, (616) 784-0058, dunnebackfarm.com, e-mail dunnebackfruit@aol.com. Family owned since 1925, Ed's daughter, Suanne Dunneback Shoemaker, specializes in strawberries, cherries, apples, squash, tomatoes, pumpkins, honey; also corn maze, bakehouse pastries.

Pleasant Hill Blueberry Farm, 5859 124th Ave., Fennville MI 49408, (269) 561-2850, pleasanthillblueberryfarm.org. For 30-plus years, John Van Voorhees and Joan Donaldson grow organic blueberries at Pleasant Hill Farm, one of the first certified organic blueberry farms in Michigan.

Eater's Guild Farm: 26041 County Road 681, Bangor MI 49013, (269) 427-0423, eatersguild.com, e-mail contact@eatersguild.com. Organic vegetable growers Lee and Laurie Arboreal farm 40 acres in a Community Supported Agriculture (CSA) program; in the Black River watershed within the Lake Michigan fruit belt of southwest Michigan. One of the first farms settled in the region.

Trillium Haven Farm: 1391 Maplewood Drive, Jenison MI 49428, (616) 457-5822, trilliumhavenfarm.com, e-mail trilliumhaven@earthlink.net. Owners Michael Vanderbrug and Anja Mast produce vegetables grown without chemical fertilizers or pesticides; also handcrafted products at an on-farm store open Saturdays.

Brother Nature Produce: facebook.com/pages/Brother-Nature-Produce: In Corktown, Detroit's oldest neighborhood, Greg Willerer farms two acres, operating Detroit's first CSA; also vends at two farmers markets, supplies eight locally owned restaurants. Willerer grows salad greens, herbs, heirloom tomatoes.

D-Town Farm: Detroit Black Community Food Security Network is located at Rogue Park at Orangelawn and Outer Drive, (313) 345-3663, detroitblackfoodsecurity.org. D-Town runs a multi-acre organic farm producing vegetables, mushrooms, beehives with hoop houses for year-round production and composting.

Greening of Detroit/Grown in Detroit: greeningofdetroit.com. 1418 Michigan Ave., Detroit, MI 48216, (313) 345-3663. Nonprofit resource agency started in 1989 as a reforesting program for the city's neighborhoods, boulevards, and parks; a collaborative of hundreds of family and community gardens totaling 80 acres with 41 fruit and vegetable varieties; Grown in Detroit is a cooperative of the city's 37 market gardens; helps support 350-plus urban gardens throughout the city.

Ann Arbor Project Grow: (734) 996-3139 projectgrowgardens.org. Identifies underdeveloped land, arranges for its use, maintains it as part of network of community gardens; also programming for children, senior citizens, gardeners with disabilities; produces organic vegetable and herb seedlings.

Light of Day Organics Farm Store: 3502 E. Traverse Hwy., Traverse City MI 49684; (231) 228-7234; lightofdayorganics.com, e-mail Orders@ LightOfDayOrganics.com.

Westwind Milling Co., 8572 Silver Lake Road, Linden MI 48451; (810) 735-9192, westwindmilling.com. Certified-organic mill and bakery, retail store 10 a.m.-6 p.m. Tuesday through Saturday, noon-5 p.m. Sunday. Lee and Linda Purdy conduct mill tours including lunch; also bread-baking mill tours; farm tours to collect chicken eggs, see heritage breed turkeys, cows, horses; also wagon ride to view crops, eat a farm cookout; freshly milled products also available at Lunasa Market, Ann Arbor's online storefront, at www.lunasa.com.

Carlson-Arbogast Farm, 4795 Reed Road, Howard City MI 49329; (231) 937-5470. Montcalm County farm grows specialty dry beans, including cranberry, kidney, mayocoba, pinto and black beans.

DeGrandchamps Farms, 76241 14th Ave., South Haven MI 49090; (888) 483-7431; degrandchamps.com. Vince and Bea DeGrandchamp started in 1958; blueberry farm near the shores of Lake Michigan now up to 130 acres, including retail market, you-pick operation; planted cranberries in 1994; nursery division one of the nation's leading blueberry nurseries; also sells in winter-hardy rhododendrons and azaleas.

FROM THE ORCHARD

Just after the summer solstice in Michigan, the wonderful weeks of orchard treasures stretch out before you all the way to the fall. The tree-ripened goodness starts with cherries and continues through apricots, peaches, plums, nectarines, apples, pears, and more. Finding fruit matured on the tree is a world apart from grabbing a bagful at the supermarket. Often, the produce at the store is picked under-ripe so it stays tough enough to ship and warehouse. So why go there, when you're living in a state with ideal geography and climate for fresh, local fruit?

Dr. Mira Danilovich, district horticulture and marketing educator with Michigan State University's Cooperative Extension Service, says it's about time Michiganders realize their state is an agricultural wonder. Mira says she meets people too often who are surprised to discover that we grow great peaches here; that they don't have to come from Georgia. Generally, there's a lot the public doesn't know about this state, and espe-

cially about its national standing as a food producer. With the huge challenges of the manufacturing sector—from autos to appliances and office furniture—Michigan would do well to educate its citizens more about one of its other key industries. Agriculture, including apple, peach, and cherry production, pumps billions of dollars (over $71 billion in 2009) into the state economy.

The local food movement is proving to be a great way to get the word out, too, Mira says. "We're seeing people reject the fruit in the supermarket, because it is picked (prematurely) so it can be shipped across state lines and even borders. Many people don't know what an apple or a peach tastes like at the prime of ripeness, because the supermarkets value fruits that have a shelf life; that they don't have to worry about."

Speaking of ripeness, on the tree-fruits leg of our Culinary Roadtrip, we head to Red and Carol Christofferson's orchard in Ludington. It's early summer; a perfect time to taste Flamin' Fury peaches, a variety developed by private breeder Paul Friday in his Benton Harbor laboratory. Red is proud as a papa of his peaches: "We only select the very best to take to market. We can never just dump them out onto a table; we set each one out like an egg." One variety, he says, is so juicy and big that some can weigh almost two pounds.

Red also says he's an ardent believer in the gospel according to Paul Friday—and to Annette Bjorge, also a renowned peach breeder in southwestern Michigan. And talk about a breakthrough: The Flamin' Fury ripens from early July into September, so growers can offer peaches continuously at the their farmstand or market without waiting for the next variety to ripen. There's always a Flamin' Fury that's ready, Red says.

"Nothing compares to a ripe and ready peach, though," Red says as he cruises his Ludington orchard in a golf cart. Red, a geologist by training, moved from chilly Saskatchewan, Canada, years ago. With his wife, Carol, a Peterson of the Peterson Farms, the largest privately owned fruit processor in Michigan, he established Maple Hill Farms, where they grow peaches, apricots, nectarines, plums, apples, blackberries, green table grapes, and Christmas trees.

The combination of soil and climate around Lake Michigan shore's famed fruit belt provides prime conditions for growing stone fruit—cherries, peaches, apricots, plums, and nectarines. In the 1780's, the first peach tree was planted in Berrien County, which, by the mid nineteen century. became synonomous with peach production and grew to become one of the country's great fruit-growing regions. Since the 1940s, Michigan's Haven series, created by Michigan State University's peach breeding program in South Haven, led the way in modern-day peach production.

Red and Carol, both knowledgeable orchardists, regularly cruise through the orchards, checking progress of their Flamin' Fury, Stellar, Redhavens, doughnut-shaped peaches called Peento, and white-fleshed varieties that are a pleasure but too delicate to ship very far. In 1993, when Red retired from teaching high school, the couple diversified their fruit orchard to 20 peach varieties and expanded to 40 acres of fruit on their 120-acre farm. A few years ago, they got into a few interspecies varieties, including the aprium, (part apricot and part peach), developed in California.

"We decided to have a little more fun," Red says. Also interspersed here are seedless Hemrod grapes, a thornless blackberry called Apache, and an early apple called Zestar. Of the Hemrods, Carol says, "I wanted a green seedless grape, similar to a grocery-store grape, but with more flavor."

Fruit farming takes patience. It is a while— four to five years—before a tree will bear anything marketable. Pruning is an endless chore, and all the while the orchardist must anticipate trouble before it comes a-knocking. Red (the nickname was from his ice-hockey days as a Michigan State Spartan) cares for his orchard with integrated pest

management techniques, including surgical, preventive pruning, fungicide use only when necessary, and the use of natural pheromone strips. These practices are part of Red's overall low-impact strategy for controlling orchard disease.

A few years ago, the Christoffersons noticed that many people want to understand the food system better and even want to go to an orchard and harvest the fruit themselves. Now, the couple has an open-door policy on the picking operation, so people are able to stop by and take part in the harvest. The couple's brick Victorian home, surrounded by lovely gardens, also has become a destination for weddings.

"When they come out, they keep saying thank you, thank you, thank you. I say, well, you're paying for it. Why thank me?" Red says with a smile.

Cherry of a business

The McManus brothers—George, Arthur and Michael—carry on a farming legacy that stretches back 140 years in northern Michigan. It all started when their great-great-grandfather, James McManus, stepped off a tall ship at Bowers Harbor on Old Mission Peninsula from Quebec in 1867. Over time, McManus and his

clan became cherry farmers on that beautiful finger of Great Lakes land, and today the brothers farm about 900 acres of cherries from Traverse City to the Leelanau Peninsula.

The picturesque rises and the Lake Michigan breeze that rolls over them are perfect for cherry orchards. Warm air swirling around the bay moderates the temperature and keeps frost away from springtime buds, while the sandy soil is just right for the roots. That combination of high ground, good drainage and moderate microclimate helps produce first-rate cherries. At the McManus orchards, the season starts shortly after the Fourth of July, with the early fruiting Caliver variety. Harvests continue through August if the conditions are right, with Hudsons and Schnieders showing up late to the party.

"We're not smart enough to get out," jokes brother George. "Really, we grew up in the business; it's part of us."

Michigan grows the most tart cherries of any state. In fact, we grow about three-quarters of all the nation's tart cherries. Though it might sound like everyone has cherry growing down pat, that doesn't make the job easy. It's far from it. In 2010, spring frosts killed most of the early buds, even on higher ground. Production was down by about 47 percent for tart cherries, which came in at about 140 million pounds, according to the Michigan Agricultural Statistics Service. The sweet cherry harvest was 41 percent below the 2009 production.

McManus family members dabbled in "local food" before it was a cool catch phrase. They ran roadside stands in the 1950s and '60s and, later, two bustling retail markets, complete with bakery and cherry-pitting equipment. The brothers' kids grew up, graduated from college, and started careers in the city, so they turned to the commercial market for many years. Eventually, though, Arthur's daughter-in-law LeWay, who grew up in Manila, in the Philippines, decided to reopen the McManus Southview Orchards you-pick operation. Today, they grow—and you can pick —the dark Bing

types called hearty giants, plus Ulster, Hedelfingen, and light-colored varieties such as Emperor Francis and Gold, just to name a few. Most of the tart cherries are Montmorency and Balaton.

The enterprising, soft-spoken LeWay recalls that it just seemed right to return the McManus family farm to its local connections. She had a feeling that people were hungry for tree-ripened cherries and getting to know their local farmers.

"When I was pregnant with my son, Arthur, people made stuff for the baby. They brought me so many gifts," says LeWay, who also has a daughter, McKenzie, with her husband, Todd McManus. "They wanted to kind of connect with me and my family. So now they know what happens (at an orchard) when it's

too warm and the trees blossom; when the frost takes it away; when the cherries are late."

LeWay's husband likes the business, too. "People can really appreciate how pretty it is out here (in the orchards)," Todd says. "We've got a little view of the bay. Go up on that hill a little further. Then you can see both bays and the peninsula."

Apple state of mind

For the state's three "antique apple" growers, an apple is never just an apple. But that's probably to be expected from people with such a passion for one of Michigan's truly trademark products.

At working orchards in Eau Claire, Midland, and Northport, orchardists grow a treasury of rare apple varieties, some with orange flesh or the taste of pumpkin, and some with popularity dating back centuries. Wonderful variety names abound, including the Green New Pippen (from the 1700s), Tolman's Sweet (circa 1820s), Roxbury russet, and Esopus Spitzenburg, Thomas Jefferson's favorite. Yes, the people behind these orchards are passionate about their apples. Actually, the resurgence of interest in high-quality apples follows several decades of decline. Years ago, farmers along Lake Michigan's shoreline grew hundreds of apple varieties, sold fresh and milled into cider, but big supermarkets eventually pushed out the little guy to sell perfect-looking but barely flavored Red Delicious and their ilk.

Thank goodness our taste buds finally revolted, because now the choices are better than ever. On the Leelanau Peninsula, John Kilcherman's Christmas Cove Farm is a case in point. Should John, who is 80, take you into his heirloom apple orchards, you could see dozens of varieties you've never heard of, let alone tasted.

On a visit to Christmas Cove, John touts the many choices. "Calville Blancs. The Blanc is a very old apple, from Normandy, in France, dating back to the 1600s," he says. "Calville Blanc is the apple you always see in those French paintings, along with a bottle of wine and grapes."

> "The Lady apple goes back to the Caesars, about two thousands years ago."

John moves on to another tree. "The Lady apple goes back to the Caesars, about two thousands years ago," he says of a variety developed by the Etruscans. It is wonderfully teeny, about 1½ inches in diameter. Perfect for holiday decorating, such as wreathes, centerpieces, fruit topiaries, place settings. It is said that royal ladies of the 17th century French court kept Lady apples in their pockets to crunch for a quick breath freshener.

"Wagoner is a real old apple that keeps a long time," John says. "The Wagoner, crossed with Jonathan, is one of the parents of the Ida Red."

"Sheep's nose, also called a Black Gilliflower, has a long pointed shape like the nose of a sheep," John said. "See, it has got a funny shape. It kind of comes to a point."

"Baldwin. It was the second leading variety in America at the turn of the century. Back then, in the 1900s, apples had a different value," John says. "Back then, before refrigeration, it was the keeping quality of an apple that was most important. So the Baldwin, a bright-red winter apple, was a good keeper (and very popular)."

"Opalascent looks so polished and pretty that people have asked me if I polish them," John says. "No, that's how they come off the tree. Some consider the Opalascent the prettiest of all apples."

At Christmas Cove Farm, John, and his wife, Phyllis, grow more than 240 varieties of heirloom apples. Some use the term "antique" apples because they are treasures from yesteryears. For more than century, John's family has farmed this gorgeous peninsula point —a picturesque tip of old world farms and orchards surrounded by Lake Michigan and Grand Traverse Bay. John grew up among these trees and even carved out a baseball diamond once in a thinning orchard. For the makeshift diamond, a winter "banana" apple served as the children's first base, a snow apple was second, and an Egremont russet was third, John recalls. The pitcher's mound and home plate? They were spots where trees had declined and been pulled. In another story of the old days, John and Phyllis both say the oldest apple tree on the property is an early-blooming yellow transparent planted by John's grandfather, who immigrated from Switzerland in 1884.

On the September Sunday that my husband, Rich, and our son, Nico, visit the Kilchermans, about 80 varieties are available for purchase in the barn. Want something unusual? Try the Russian-bred Duchess of Oldenburg (circa 1700s), the white-fleshed Snow White, sunset-hued Pumpkin Sweet, Turkish Kandel Sinep, or the Westfield Seek-No-Further.

Or, if seeking further, try Yellow Newtown Pippin, sometimes called George Washington's favorite (circa 1750); Brock, a Golden Delicious and McIntosh cross (1933, from Maine); or Colonel Ashmead, a very old English russet that's not the prettiest apple in the bushel but sure tastes good.

Phyllis says she has a couple of favorites: the Ingrid Marie, discovered off the coast of Denmark, and the Isle of Fyn, believed to be a descendant of the Orange Pippin.

The farm runs a thriving mail-order operation, with 12- and 16-apple boxes attractively packaged for gifting, complete with printed histories for each variety in the box. For fresh product in the barn, they make it a point to label each apple variety, scouring old books and catalogs to discover its history. Then Phyllis takes it one step further by cooking with the many varieties—pies, crisps, crumbles, applesauce, chutney, spice cakes—so she knows thoroughly how that variety behaves in the kitchen.

Later on, pears and chestnuts

The American pear story, shared less often than Johnny Appleseed's, reveals many fragrant varieties besides the canning darling Bartlett. Michigan fruit farms these days are raising tree-ripened, yellow-brown Clapp's Favorite, winter darling Anjou, russet-skinned Comice, sweet melting Eldorado, and a true American pear, Seckel, that I first tasted at the Traverse City farmers market in 2008.

Mari and Chris Reijmerink of Fennville decided to restore an old pear orchard, bringing it back into production with organic methods. Far from uniform in size, shape, and color, the gnarly-looking pear trees now yield crazy-good Barlett, Bosc and Clapp's Favorite varieties. The heirloom Clapp's, from the 1860s, have a large, thick-skinned fruit that is almost buttery tasting.

Each year, beginning around Labor Day, the Reijmerinks harvest the pears and sell most of them to regular customers and a few at market. These pears are so sweet and buttery that when you mix all three and simmer them together, they make a divine pear sauce, similar to applesauce. "I make a pear vanilla cake that is tender and rich, with farm eggs," says Mari, who is building a community-supported bakery on the farm.

The all-organic orchard is managed in some very old-fashioned ways. Mari and Chris are always on the lookout for trouble in the orchard, for damage from bugs or signs of disease.

"We're trying to be environmentally responsible," Mari says. "We believe good pest management has to come from the earth and go back to the earth. There are beneficial and harmful flora and fauna all around us; the trick is keeping it in balance. We mostly use nutrients and beneficial bacteria and fungi to keep the plants healthy, which makes for stronger plants. If you think of every leaf as real estate, then we're just being responsible landlords. We try to keep the space full of good fungi and bacteria and make sure nutrients are available to the plant. Then, there's no room for the bad guys and they can't move in," she says.

The Reijmerinks have another fine product of the orchard on their farm south of Holland. Their grove of chestnut trees, including Chinese, European, and Japanese varieties, is a dreamy place. A visitor can easily imagine fine ladies clothed in Victorian gowns, parasols, and white gloves playfully hiding about. The chestnut tree, spiky with green, single-barbed burrs, looks all the world like a scene from a "Masterpiece Theater" presentation. "It's quite a little grove," Mari says. "Go right into the middle, and it's grassy and shady. I swear the fairies live in here.

"Chestnuts are a very nostalgic for Americans," she says. Generally, all of Mari's chestnuts are spoken for, but try the Michigan Chestnut Growers Inc., a producer co-op with 37 members. The growers roast fresh chestnuts and sell chestnut products at a handful of locations (Detroit's Eastern Market, Royal Oak farmers market, an East Lansing location) around the holidays. Find the chestnut co-op at www.chestnutgrowers.com. Ready-to-use, vacuum-sealed chestnuts are available at the site, along with grower addresses, recipes, and events.

Between seasons, there's syrup

Between winter's end and spring's birth, sugar maple trees usher in the state's first crop of the year: maple syrup. Delivering more than sweetness, maple syrup signals that the brutally cold days of midwinter are passing. For centuries, the First People throughout the region collected sap from sugar maple trees to sweeten their provisions in the toughest, leanest food days of the year. They cut a gash in the tree, collected the sap in birchbark buckets, then boiled it down to the amber gold that is 100-percent pure maple syrup. Not that different from how it's done today.

Today, Michigan maple syrup is made simply and traditionally by some, in sparkling modern facilities by others. The modernized operations use technological precision, including special tubing, vacuum pumps, and reverse osmosis filters.

When the sap runs in late winter, Cheboygan's Lowell Beethem is one of the many small-scale sugar-makers scattered around the state sending up clouds of steam from family sugar shacks out in the woods.

Only a few snowy places in North America, especially in parts of Canada, the Great Lakes region, and New England (Vermont being the largest producer), have the right soil conditions to allow sugar maples to prosper in groves and the right weather conditions to have a good, sudden sap flow as winter breaks. When the day-time highs hit the 30s but the nights are still cold, pressure changes inside sugar maples force sap to flow —which is where Lowell comes in.

Lowell trudges through waist-high snow to poke his sugar maples and connect tubing lines that carry the flow-ing sap to a 1,500-gal-lon tank near his sugar shack. From that holding station, Lowell pumps it into a tank on the back

> ## "My maple syrup benefits from the wood smoke curling around it."

of his truck and transfers it to an elevated unit in his syrup-making shed. From there, gravity trickles the water-thin sap into a evaporator. Lowell boils—and boils and boils—the sap in a wide, 14-foot-long, wood-fired trough. That's it. After a while, it's pure maple syrup. It's a lot of work, considering it takes 40 gallons of the sap for one gallon of the product. Lowell and his family spends long spring days and nights stoking their wood-fire, dodging the smoke, and toiling through the steam.

"I'm not running my maple sap through a re-verse osmosis machine, which takes out 80 percent of the water and reduces the boiling in half," says Lowell, a retired Cheboygan middle school teacher. "And I don't boil the sap with fuel oil or propane. I don't want to; it takes away from flavor. My maple syrup benefits from the wood smoke curling around it. People tell me it's the only syrup they will buy, and they come for it year after year."

Around here, sugaring is a family social event, with everyone visiting the steamy, sweet-smelling shack at some point during the short season to monitor the boiling or throw some wood on the fire. For many fami-lies like the Beethems, syrup season is a tra-dition that spans the generations.

When Lowell was a boy of nine, living in Cheboygan, his dad worked during the week downstate in Drayton Plains, near Detroit. With a bunch of his dad's ma-ple-syrup equipment— buckets, spiles, braces, and bit—laying around, young Lowell grabbed a hammer and went after few sugar maples. Then

he hung a bucket onto each spile and covered it with a lid to keep out snow, rain, bugs, and squirrels. "I brought the sap into the house, put it on my mother's wood stove, and made some syrup. She kicked me out (of the kitchen) after I peeled the wallpaper off the walls from the moisture from the sap. The next year, I set up an old witch's kettle, you know what I mean, the big black kettle, and put that across a log and hung that over the fire."

By the time, he was 19, he rigged a broken-down pickup into a makeshift sugaring operation, complete with an onboard woodstove, chimney, and flat pan. Lowell's sugaring operation has grown from 20 trees in 1956 to 2,000 today, producing about 250 gallons of syrup per year. He also turns the sap into maple cream, by taking the sap to 232 Fahrenheit on a candy thermometer, at which points he whips until it sets. "Some call it maple butter, because it spreads like butter and is excellent on biscuits, toast,

cornbread, or anything you want a little sweetness on," Lowell says.

To make maple candy, Lowell takes the sap to 242 degrees to pour into maple-leaf-shaped molds. "There's really nothing like real maple syrup. Nothing should be added," says Lowell, who sells his products at his family home, local farmers markets, and several roadside stands in the Mackinac Straits area.

"Making maple syrup seems to be something that gets in one's blood, even though there is not much money to be made with it," he says. "A maple producer can't seem to not make syrup in the springtime, when the sun comes out and the days warm up."

Christmas Cove Farm: 11573 Kilcherman Road, on Grand Traverse Bay. Online applejournal.com/christmascove, or (231) 386-5637. Started in the 1970s; John and Phyllis Kilcherman grow more than 240 varieties of heirloom apples; they also run a mail-order operation; open from mid-September until November.

Tree Mendus Fruit Farms: 9351 E. Eureka Road, Eau Claire, (877) 863-3276 treemendusfruit.com. More than 230 varieties of antique apples at this 450-acre working farm, preserved by curator Herb Teichman from a collection of oldtime varieties, including Margil, Fallwater/Tulpenhocken, Holiday, and Golden Russet. Three types of cider made at Tree Mendus: cherry apple, dark apple, and heritage cider. Also RentATree opportunities (prices from $20 to $150, depending on size, variety). How it works: You pick a tree, the orchard staff performs all normal care, and in the fall, you come back to harvest your apples.

Eastman's Antique Apples: 1058 W. Midland-Gratiot County Line Road, Wheeler, MI 48662; (989) 842-5576 or (989) 854-6264. Cindy and Tom Ward own and operate her family's antique apple orchard, with more than 4,000 trees and hundreds of varieties. Sons, Casey and Rafe help sell Knobbed Russet, the ugliest apple in the world; Kandil Sinap, the Turkish apple shaped like a candle; Golden Nugget and King of the Pippin, for making great cider; and Flower of Kent, the apple that fell to the ground when Sir Issac Newton discovered gravity. Eastman's apples are at the Midland farmers market on Wednesday and Saturday in season.

Christofferson Farms: 3441 Morton Road, Ludington, MI 49431; (231) 845-5831, email at 2hattrick@carrinter.net. The small family-owned and operated orchard specializes in top-quality tree-ripened fruit, including peaches, plums, nectarines, apricots and apples, plus blackberries, grapes, and Christmas trees. Open 9 a.m.-5 p.m. July through September. Please call first.

Kismet Fruit Farm & Bakery: 1776 68th Street Fennville, Michigan 49408 www.kismetorganics.com. Mari and Chris Reijmerink farm 23 acres in Allegan County, raising organic fruit, select vegetables, and laying hens. The farm is certified organic. The Bakery (opening June 2012) produces pastry rich with their farm's fruit and hearth baked,crusty loaves. Their offerings are available at the farm's Road stand, check the web site for opening date and seasonal hours.

McManus Southview Orchards: 313 Garfield Road North, Traverse City, MI 49684. Open seven days a week, 9 a.m.-5 p.m. Pick or purchase cherries from mid-July through early August. At the McManus marketplace, find a wide variety of locally grown fruits and vegetables, including apples, cherries, sweet corn, onions, pumpkins, raspberries, tomatoes and winter squash.

FROM THE WATER

—◆—

Here's a special roadtrip for a seafood lover: Drive north, then cross the Mackinac Bridge and beyond, sampling wild-caught whitefish, lake trout, and smoked chubs along the way. Wondrous whitefish fillets await, grilled with a squeeze of lemon, a drizzle of olive oil, a sprinkling of fresh herbs. Or enjoy it deep-fried with a light, crispy crust. Michigan's 11,000 lakes, including the four surrounding Great Lakes, boast many a fertile fishing spot to serve up delicious, fresh-caught dinners.

The 'First People' and their fish

Native American tribes and their whitefish harvests are part of a tradition that dates back centuries. The Mackinac Straits area, connecting lakes Michigan and Huron, has long been a special place for Michigan's first people and their love of good food from the water. Long before French traders and Jesuit missionaries arrived in the late 1600s, the Anishinabek, the original people, gathered communities near cold waters teeming with whitefish, lake trout, and other species important to their livelihood, says Lisa Craig Brisson, an independent museum consultant and history educator well-versed in the state's agricultural and culinary traditions.

"For the Europeans, wild-caught whitefish was unlike any other fish they had tasted," Lisa says, "and they launched commercial fishing (in northern Michigan), shipping barrels of salted whitefish to Detroit, Chicago and Milwaukee. By the 1840s, the commercial industry had taken over, and the tribes weren't the economic beneficiaries."

A century and a half later, Michigan's Native Americans regained their fishing rights. In 2000, a consent decree recognized and affirmed tribal rights under the Treaty of 1836 to fish in expansive waters of the three upper Great Lakes. The decree, in effect through 2020, was signed by the Bay Mills Indian Community, Grand Traverse Band of Ottawa and Chippewa Indians, Little River Band of Ottawa Indians, Little Traverse Bay Bands of Odawa Indians, the Sault Ste. Marie Tribe of Chippewa Indians, the state of Michigan, and the federal government.

Still a prized catch

In shops and restaurants throughout the state, wild-caught lake fish is a special commodity, but the 1959 opening of the St. Lawrence Seaway complicated the ecological balance of the Great Lakes by introducing a wave of invasive species. Among the more than 180 newcomers are zebra mussels, which devour plankton and clog water-intake structures, and the round gobie fish, which aggressively competes with native species. Now, the voracious, invasive Asian carp (big mouth and silver) threatens the

Great Lakes basin if it succeeds in slipping through Chicago's shipping canals into Lake Michigan and beyond.

Kevin Dean, whose Superior Fish shop in Royal Oak cuts and processes more than 20,000 pounds of fresh fish and seafood a week, depends on a healthy Great Lakes system for his livelihood. "We are personally stewards of the Great Lakes," Kevin says. "It is an ecosystem that is ever-changing. Lake smelt was once so popular. In the day, everyone would go smelting, sit on the shore with trash cans, and take trash cans of fresh smelt out. Not anymore. It seems it takes more work, equipment and energy to catch the same amount of fish."

When you're ready for some great Michigan fish, though, there are plenty of places to find it, including in the big city. One example: Gorgeous, flash-frozen fillets from the cold, clear waters of the Upper Great Lakes can be found at the Fulton Street Farmers Market in Grand Rapids. Mark Schaub, from Kingsley, near Traverse City, sells from a booth most Saturdays, displaying high-quality fish processed and vacuum-packed at the Mackinac Straits Fish Co. facility in St. Ignace. Mark, who is also a poultry farmer, works with Jill Benting of Mackinac Straits Fish Company. She takes his free-range chickens and eggs and he gets her premium fish fillets and line of smoked fish products.

Jill's Mackinac Straits company annually sells more than 900,000 pounds of Great Lakes trout, whitefish, and walleye, so she knows what she's doing. And in the fine art of fish-buying, that's an important point: Always go to a trusted source; especially a location that is nice and busy, doing lots of volume and moving fresh, moist product out the door.

In the U.P. town of Naubinway, just 45 minutes west of the Mackinac Bridge, on U.S. 2, is King's Fish Market. This fishing village, in the middle of the nation's largest fresh-water reservoir, is where Bob King's family built a life around fishing. It goes back to when his great-grandfather put a single-mast sailboat, called

a mackinaw, into Lake Michigan a long time ago. "He was one of the first to settle the area," says Bob, whose identity and history in the Sault Ste. Marie Tribe of Chippewa Indians gives him a sense of belonging that stretches back hundreds of years. His people settled the area along the St. Marys River that later would become the city of Sault Ste. Marie. With his Native American ancestry clearly established, Bob holds a tribal license giving him the right to fish in a wide nautical region around Naubinway. Along with his sons, Kenny and Theron, Bob catches whitefish, lake trout, and salmon.

"It gets in your blood. I guess we are like farmers," Bob says. "When you are a farmer, you are a farmer forever. When you are a fisherman, you are a fisherman forever."

On a late fall day, Bob is busy with his boats on the wharf at Naubinway. On the fishing tug he runs, with an enclosed cabin as cozy as a little house, the crew hauls in thousands of pounds of whitefish. Bob fishes **year-round except during November spawning, always day trips that start early and get the crews home before dark. Bob also uses an open type** trap-net boat, but not in winter, when the decking might ice over. In good weather, the trap nets head out at 4:30 a.m., "when the lake is calm and cool. Before it heats up, we pack the fish and get it cooler-ready to ship out on refrigerated trucks," Bob explains. Most of Bob King's catch, which he estimates at 2 million pounds in 2010, goes to a distributor in New York. Superior Seafood, a Grand Rapids-area distributor, sends some of the haul to retail outlets in Michigan.

Wherever it goes, it's good stuff. "My wife, Beverly, makes a good fish soup," Bob says. "Call her tomorrow, and she'll give you some."

At age 69, Bob took to the water only once in 2010, but he still loves fishing the Great Lakes. "We've been doing this for six generations. I've been on this dock, my dad's dock, my whole life. I'm not as active as I used to be. Now I like to be on shore and let the boys go out."

Speaking of the "boys," son Theron has opened his own shop, in tiny Moran, just north of the Straits, where he offers fresh and smoked fish, spreads, and a delicious Great Lakes fish chowder from a recipe that has sustained his family through six generations.

Sure thing on the shoreline

On a beautiful stretch of Lakeshore Drive, between Ludington and Pentwater, with nice glimpses of Lake Michigan as you tool along, watch for an unassuming sign with a painted fish on it. That's Bortell's Fish Shack. Nothing much to it, really; a low, cinderblock building so crowded inside with customers we have to wait our turn outside the front screen door. Bortell's is only open Memorial Day through Labor Day, and this being the end of the season, it seems everyone has come for a last taste of summer. Once inside, we check out the selection of lake fish fillets ready to be deep-fried on the spot or packaged to go.

My husband, Rich, orders our perch and walleye, lightly seasoned and crispy-good, plus fries, coleslaw, and cans of RC Cola. This place may be barebones, with only a smattering of picnic tables outside, but those in the know say "Go!" They also suggest you bring your own party, with extra fixings, maybe a salad, some wine or beer. Skip the formalities, but bring the picnic basket.

Cross Village to Mackinaw City

In a mid-August stop at Legs Inn in Cross Village, we take an outside table and admire the view, perched on a bluff overlooking Lake Michigan. Legs Inn is known far and wide for its spectacular views, whitefish, traditional Polish plates and mom-and-pop friendliness. Owners George and Kathy Smolak handle every facet of the business, regularly visiting with diners

and tending a kitchen vegetable garden right on hand to ensure fresh-to-the-table goodness. The Smolaks specialize in fresh, wild-caught fish from Big Stone Bay Fishery. Try the whitefish blackened, broiled or part of a Straits platter. It's all good.

Taking up Kathy Smolak on her suggestion to stop by Big Stone Bay Fishery, we head to Mackinaw City. Hitting the store shortly before 9 a.m., a clerk is preparing for the day's flood of customers. "The crowds start at 9, and it's nonstop from then on," he says. As he prepares smoked whitefish sausage (sweet Italian and Cajun), we gawk at the abundance of fish—whole, fillet, smoked, sausage, and spread. In the back of the building, we can see the crew carrying out important jobs, from cleaning and trimming fish to boxing them onto the fishery's fleet of large, white delivery trucks.

Everything in the cases at Big Stone Bay—the whitefish, trout, walleye, smelt, perch, chubs—looks bright, shiny, and firm. They smell like the lake, not fishy or sour. I load up on the variety, including the smoked whitefish spread (more than 2,000 containers a week sold here), and they pack the goodies solid with ice for our trip home.

Charlevoix picturesque streets might be bumper-to-bumper busy in midsummer vacation mode, but inside **John Cross Fisheries**, June Cross serenely picks out golden chunks of smoked whitefish for her eager clientele. "It's smoked in maple wood," she says. "One of the cleanest woods there is."

June, the wife of Jack Cross, makes all of the store's signature creamy spread, full of moist chunks of smoked fish, fresh lemon juice, and the secret ingredients that make it divine. Some weeks, she can't make the batches fast enough. "Come back in about an hour," she tells one hopeful customer. "We can't keep up with the demand."

John Cross Fisheries, since 1954

In constant motion, daughter Kellie Sutherland and granddaughter Megan Cross hop from front-counter sales to the production side, seeing to the needs of every person who crosses the threshold. "We give people the best fish that we can find," June says.

John Cross, June's father-in-law, started the business in 1954. One of 15 children, John was born on Beaver Island, and at age 16 he struck out on his own, fishing in lakes Michigan, Superior, and Huron and selling his catch at the Charlevoix fish market. Later, his son Jack also fished until the 2000 federal consent decree returned the area's commercial fishing rights to Native Americans. Now Jack and June work with the tribal fisheries to supply product to restaurants, retail customers, and wholesalers.

"We give people the best fish that we can find."

Behind the store, the Cross family operates a processing facility. Granddaughter Megan conducts a tour: "The boats come right in here—this is Charlevoix Bay—and bring us the fish." Surveying the scene, fresh catch is everywhere. Workers bustle around in waders, standing on a concrete floor, swiftly and efficiently cleaning and packing about 600 pounds every day. "Sometimes it feels like this is the most popular place in the world," says Megan as her grandpa, Jack, is spotted returning from a delivery. "It can get crazy."

In Royal Oak, at **Superior Fish Company,** customers cluster three-deep around the counter. This business, a longtime presence across the street from the local farmers market, operates out of an unremarkable red-brick bunker of a building. But talk about busy. On Saturdays, the owners' daughters pass out samples of

grilled whitefish fillets seasoned with smoke and fire. A perfect taste of the Great Lakes can be found inside, with the fish shop emphasizing wild-caught rather than farm-raised product.

Perched on piles of crushed ice, all manner of whitefish are fanned out, including whole ones with tight, shiny scales, fillets with moist, translucent skin, and smoked ones with a golden hue from smoldering hardwood. Superior Fish Company is celebrating 70 years under Dean family ownership (now Kevin and David Dean). Their father, John, had worked in the

business since he caught frog legs on Lake St. Clair as a youth.

"We're very fortunate to be in a Great Lakes state," says Kevin, wandering about to chat with customers and answer their questions. "Fresh lake whitefish is part of our heritage; like if you went to California, you would have Pacific snapper. If you were to go to Florida, you would have grouper. The East Coast, you would be eating blue crabs."

Technically speaking, not everything we find is wild-caught or even native to these lakes. For the excit-

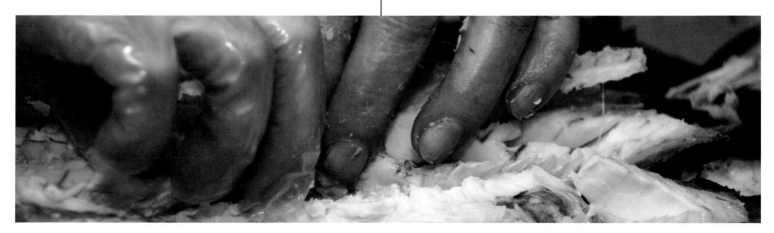

ing and new, look for homegrown Michigan shrimp.

Seriously; shrimp. In Okemos, east of Lansing, Shrimp Farm Market (theshrimpmarket.com) bills itself as the first commercially producing indoor shrimp farm in the world, pioneered by Russ Allen. The store, at 3450 Meridian Road, in Okemos, is open 11 a.m. to 6 p.m. Friday, 10 a.m. to 1 p.m. Saturday. The Fish Market keeps winter hours at Meridian Mall Winter Market on the second Saturday (10 a.m.-3 p.m.) of each month from December until April.

King's Fish Market, Two locations – 11501 W. Lake St., Naubinway, MI 49762; (906) 477-6362 and (906) 477-6282; and M-123 Moran, MI 49760; (906) 643-1068. Bob King and his sons, Kenny and Theron. Sample the wild-caught lake fish at Kings Market in two U.P. locations, both serving tasty grub.

Bortell's Fisheries, 5528 S. Lakeshore Drive, Ludington MI 49431; (231) 843-3337. Only open Memorial Day through Labor Day. Named one of America's Top 10 seafood shacks, Bortell got its start in 1898 with German Uriah Bortell.

Legs Inn, 6425 N. Lake Shore Drive, Cross Village, MI 49723; (231) 526-2281; www.legsinn.com. Restauranteurs George and Kathy Smolak count on fresh wild-caught fish from Big Stone Bay Fishery. The scenic Polish restaurant's blackened Great Lakes whitefish, broiled Great Lakes whitefish, walleye – the catch of the day, Straits whitefish platter and smoked whitefish appetizer with homemade rye bread, is a tasty testimony that local is better.

Big Stone Bay Fishery, 10975 US Highway -23, Mackinaw City, MI 49701; (231) 436-4144. Owner Cameron McMurry took to fishing like no other. At his operation, the crew cleans, fillets, packages and delivers all the live-long summer days. Check out his fish spread.. During tourist season, it doesn't stay long.

John Cross Fisheries, 209 Belvedere Ave., Charlevoix, MI 49720; (231) 547-2532. Back in 1954, John Cross, started the business. Later, his son, Jack Cross, pursued fishing until 2000. Now Jack and June Cross concentrate on working with trusted sources to provide independent restaurants, customers, and wholesalers with wild-caught Great Lakes fish.

Superior Fish Company, 309 E. 11 Mile Road, Royal Oak MI, 48068; (248) 541-4632; www.superiorfish.com. The full-service fish market. The Dean family continues to share the best of the Great Lakes, emphasizing wild-caught.

FROM THE DAIRY BARN

As much as it is a refreshing glass of goodness from a cow, modern milk also is a high-tech product. The ultra-high-temperature pasteurized (UHP) milk in today's supermarket coolers is a case in point. Its makers, not the cows, the factory folks, super-sterilize the milk so they can ship it great distances and keep it "on shelf" for weeks. Such a powerfully processed dairy product is a far cry from what many small farmers are trying to provide for the thoughtful local-food consumer.

> "This is nearly a forgotten taste."

So-called cream-line milk (a term for non-homogenized product that proponents say tastes better and is better for you) is in demand these days because many are trying to eat foods closer to their "natural" state, with less processing. The less the farmer and manufacturer monkey around with the product, the more wholesome it is. Or so the thinking goes. Non-homogenized milk is only one food-safety step (it's usually pasteurized) away from raw milk, making it a logical choice for many of today's simple-foods advocates.

While Michigan takes pride in a wonderful dairy heritage going way back, this Culinary Roadtrip chapter on dairy focuses on the very small operations in the state that milk their own animals, process the product in small batches, and truck it to local outlets such as markets, co-ops, and restaurants.

"This is nearly a forgotten taste," says Connie Straathof of Hilhof Dairy in Hersey, near Reed City. "Many haven't tasted milk like this, especially the younger generation. Our milk is like a medicine; it is healing. People, who have been lactose intolerant, who haven't drunk milk for years, can drink ours. People thank us because they can finally drink milk again."

For "locavores," those who strive to eat food grown and produced in the region where they live, micro-creameries selling directly to the consumer are right up their alley. And finally, after economies of scale have knocked off so many small businesses, some of these enterprises are making a go of it. For Connie and her husband, William, though, it was a very long leap of faith into this business. Things weren't so great when they first tried to sell their milk.

"I came to Grand Rapids with a full truck two weeks in a row and came home with a full load, because I couldn't find a store to sell the milk. They didn't want anything to do with milk in bottles," William says. "We finally got into Kingma's Market and then, two weeks later, we meet you (I was the Food Editor at *The Grand Rapids Press*). When you put us in the newspaper and online, boom, the stores started calling us!"

This writer remembers the Straathofs very well, and our encounter at that local market, followed by the coverage of their delicious fresh milk in old-fashioned bottles. I remember being delighted I could give my family, including our three young children, the next best thing to raw milk. And I recall the amazing taste of a tall, cold glass of cream-line milk: Refreshingly delicious, full of creamy flavor. I was used to watery skim milk, which literally pales in comparison.

Michigan's handful of micro-creameries are producing full-flavored, old-fashioned milk products including chocolate milk, cream, buttermilk, eggnog, drink-able yogurts, butter, and ice cream. And when it comes to cheese, well, we've hit the jackpot. Eleven micro-creameries have formed the Michigan Cheese Makers Cooperative to get in on the gourmet cheese market so people can choose local product for their fine dining and entertaining.

Clearly there's a new breed of farmer out there offering specialty, or niche, products that appeal to a new breed of consumer. On this dairy-product leg of our Culinary Roadtrip, we first venture to Shetler's Dairy Farm in Kalkaska, east of Traverse City. Shetler's is a fascinating small business that offers farm tours and a milk store stocked with lots of lip-smacking varieties of hand-crafted ice cream. Everything is done so well here that it's hard to believe Shetlers almost didn't make it.

Back in the mid-1990s, Sally Shetler knew the writing was on the wall. In her heart of hearts, she understood that dairy farming, something she and her husband, George, had been doing since 1979, wasn't working anymore. They were worn out and going broke.

It's not as if they hadn't kept current and put their everything into it. Their farm's soil had all the organic certifications, they raised beautiful Holsteins, Brown Swiss, Jerseys, and various crosses. They did their own hay and pulled it out when snow covered all the grazing spots on their land.

They decided to take the bull by the horns, so to speak. Sally sat down and wrote a letter to every health food store she could find in the state of Michigan. Plain and simple, she wanted to know whether the store would be interested in carrying a new Shetler's cream-line milk —a premium, glass-bottle, non-homogenized product with a thick layer of real cream on top. Yes or no; that's all she wanted to know. She was driven to this direct marketing and research to determine what was next for the family farm.

"We had to make a decision about whether we wanted to get rid of the dairy farm. We couldn't make it," says Sally. "In 1995, 40 cows couldn't support one family; that's why there are hardly any dairy farmers left. I sent the survey letter out to see if there was any interest— and there was. We actually started with 13 stores in the Traverse City area and now have about 40 stores in a 60-mile radius."

Today, more than 15 years later, the Shetlers have 180 acres and 40 cows—1,500-pound, black-and-white Holsteins, caramel-colored Jerseys, and a few Brown Swiss. They graze small sections of pasture at a time, then are rotated to a new area, giving them a diet of fresh, wholesome grasses rather than chemically laden feed. "About five percent of their feed is corn; just a little grain," Sally says. The Shetlers never give their animals growth hormones or antibiotics, and their fields are free of chemical pesticides and herbicides.

"We aren't certified organic, but my husband has been farming organically for years," Sally says. "Our land was certified organic in the 1990s, for seven years, but we dropped the certification. George is working hard to do things differently, (and) that is why we decided to bottle ourselves." She says people are welcome to visit, look around, see what they're doing. They will see they are providing care that is healthy, safe, and sound for the animals and for the consumers of their products. "It's a whole trust thing," she says.

Near the milking parlor, a dozen calves mill around their pen. "Some of these little guys are just a couple of days old," Sally says. "We noticed an umbilical cord hanging down on one of them, so that one is a brand new one." Nearby are some miniature horses somebody couldn't afford to feed so they ended up in the couple's care. "We got them for free," Sally says. Inside the parlor, the cows are milked every 12 hours (5 a.m. and 5 p.m.) in their own tie-stall. "They each know their stall and will go straight to it most of the time," Sally says.

From the cows, the milk goes into a sterile pipeline for filtering on its way to a holding tank. Next, gentle, low-temperature pasteurization retains valuable

enzymes lost in today's ultra-pasteurization process. Then the product is held for containment, done twice weekly, in glass milk bottles shipped from the only available source, in Ontario, Canada. The Shetler product line includes fat-free, reduced-fat (2 percent), and full-fat, cream-line milk, plus yogurt, smoothies, and ice cream.

Sally says they put together the bottling plant 12 years ago, partly with antique machinery, because nobody makes such equipment anymore. The bottling and bottle-washing equipment is a rarity sometimes described as antique. But everything is working just fine, she says.

Similar story in mid-Michigan

Hilhof Dairy's William and Connie Straathof trekked to Iowa for the bottle-filling and -washing equipment they needed back home in Hersey. "We had to do lots of fixing and rebuilding," William says.

At the Straathofs' Osceola County farm there are 34 Holsteins nurtured on a pure diet of organic oats and grass. More than 12 years ago, William decided to convert the farm where he had grown up into a certified-organic facility, and about four years later he received all the approvals. Soon after, he also began to bottle and sell organic, cream-line milk, and now they can barely keep up with the demand. Stores are clamoring for Hilhof Dairy from as far away as Saginaw and Kalamazoo.

William's usual Thursday deliver day goes like this: Up at 5 a.m., check the animals and load the truck; at 7 a.m. his wife, Connie, joins him, and they drive south to Kent County, where they stop first at the Gristmill in Cannonsburg. There they haul away the returns, retrieve any milk near its expiration date in the cooler and cart in the freshly bottled product. Back to the truck and off they go to the Grand Rapids area, where they will deliver to Kingma's Market, Grand Central Station, Martha's Vineyard, Cherry Hill Market, Apple Valley in Kentwood, Forest Hills Foods in Cascade Township, Grand River Grocery in Ada, Sobe Meats in Walker, and three Harvest Health stores. Pushing on, they head for the lakeshore, delivering to Saugatuck, Holland, Grand Haven, and Muskegon outlets.

> "We won't get home until 11 p.m., and then we've got to unload the truck."

"We won't get home until 11 p.m., and then we've got to unload the truck. We don't get into the house until 11:30 or midnight," William says.

"At least it's blacktop the whole way," Connie adds with a laugh.

The raw-milk debate

Some want their milk straight from the cow. For these dairy lovers, raw milk is the way to go. Problem is, in Michigan and 22 other states, you have to buy your own cow to do this, because selling unpasteurized milk directly to consumers is prohibited. Karen and Jeff Lubbers, of the Grand Rapids area, didn't set out in farming with an agenda that included raw dairy, but things just worked out that way. "We've been drinking raw milk on the farm because of Jamie's brain cancer," Karen says. "The short story is, our daughter got cancer —so we got a cow. There are a lot of blanks in there, but, yeah, that is it."

Raw-milk lovers seek out the product for its fresh taste and because it contains beneficial enzymes and bacteria that are killed by pasteurization, the process of heating milk to improve food safety and extend shelf life. The U.S. Centers for Disease Control and Prevention Public say more than 1,500 people became ill from drinking raw milk between 1993 and 2006, the most recent years for which data are available. Of the 1,500 sickened, 185 were hospitalized, and two died.

Those who consider raw milk a must-have are finding a way around the ban by joining a "herd share" program, under which the customer legally buys into a dairy herd and

owns one or more of the cows. Under these arrangements, the leaseholder brings along his or her own container to haul home the week's share of product, which is usually a few gallons on a small dairy farm. The initial dairy share can run about $200, in most cases. Karen is a big proponent: "By definition, raw milk—a living, breathing, wild food product—is a local food. We should treat it that way."

California, which has the nation's biggest raw milk industry, is one of just nine states to permit its

sale in stores. Nineteen states allow retail sales directly from the farm. Twenty-three states prohibit the sales, but seven of those are allowing the herd-share programs.

Bill Robb, a Michigan State University senior Cooperative Extension Service educator, recently retired, strongly sticks by pasteurization.

"Raw milk, cow shares; that's all very controversial," says Bill, who grew up consuming the unprocessed product on his family's farm in Fowlerville. "In fact, there is some new research that is questioning everything. E. coli and salmonella have been found in raw-milk cheese even after it has gone through the aging process. I'm not sure consumers who are (drinking) raw milk understand what's going on.

"I worked for commercial agriculture all of my career. We developed these safety procedures…to provide the most nourishing product. Pasteurized milk is a safe product, and if you want to go backward in time to a non-pasteurized product, then you take the risk that comes with it. We have a population today that wasn't raised on the farm and hasn't got the same immunity levels; if they get one of those bugs, it's going to bring them low. There are cases all across the country of where that has happened."

And the debate goes on. "Raw milk by definition comes with bacteria—good guys and bad guys," Karen says. "They both nourish us. The bad guys help our immunities. We as farmers and raw milk cheesemakers are offering a product to an immune-suppressed population, so it's kind of scary. We're raising kids in glass bubbles; the best thing that you can do is give them a spoonful of dirt!"

On their 120-acre farm near the Kent and Ottawa county line west of Grand Rapids, the Lubbers name all their cows because they stay and stay, unlike confinement dairy cows that are retired after only three or four years. The four-legged family of 14 Jerseys includes Pansy, Mikki, Heather, Mona (she moans a lot), and Pretty Penny (she was expensive). Also, the Lubbers run a farm store offering ground beef, succulent beef, whey-fed pork, eggs from the eggmobile, bread, rolls, buns and crackers (new) from their son Casey's Little Red Rooster Bakery, cheeses from the farm's creamery, honey from the farm, syrup from a friend's farm, jams and chutneys from a farm intern and culinary student, assorted flours, and some fabulous cutting boards from rescued scrap hardwoods.

In addition to the dairy cows, they raise heritage breeds of chickens and hogs, all without stimulants, synthetic additives, or hormones.

Karen and Jeff recently took another big step with their business. They figured their extra tasty, high-fat Jersey milk would make excellent cheese, so they converted a portion of their farmstead into cheese production. "July 1 (2010) was our first day of cheese-making. In this first year, we're determined to get really good, to do something really well," Karen says. "We're more interested in quality than quantity."

Jeff named the micro-creamery Cowslip after the perennial herb that sprouts up en masse on the banks of the nearby Grand River. "Cowslip is a Michigan native herb that shows up in the spring," Karen says. "And in the old days, the ancients used to celebrate the cowslip as the harbinger of spring."

Karen also loved William Shakespeare's use of the word in The Tempest: "Where the bee sucks, there suck I; In a cowslip's bell I lie." If it was good enough for The Bard himself, it was good enough for the Lubbers family.

To launch their production of raw-milk cheese, Lubbers says, she sought the advice of Neville McNaughton of CheezSorce, a nationally respected artisan-cheese consulting firm, for their plant design. She also hired Jana Deppe, a graduate of the Secchia Institute for Culinary Education and the Vermont Institute of Artisan Cheese-Making, as head cheese-maker. Jana brought to the farm a commitment to local foods as founder of Tilling-to-Table, an organization of culinary students dedicated to showing people where their food comes from.

On a recent visit to their farmstead, the Lubbers were looking forward to the release of their first Alpine Valley-style cheese, called Phocas. It is named for a second-century farmer who reached sainthood for feeding the poor and taking in travelers. To attain optimum flavor, the 12-pound wheels need to age long enough to develop a full flavor, which takes a minimum of three months in the cheese room, kept at 55 to 58 degrees and 90 percent humidity. The cheese wheels have to be smeared repeatedly with a beneficial bacteria—called a smear of cultures—to encourage the ripening process. Karen smears and flips and smears the rounds, over and over at first, then less frequently as the aging proceeds. "Yes! I'm off to smear," she says. "I will be back."

Farm-to-table dinner at Lubbers Family Farm

One gorgeous summer evening, I dine al fresco style at Lubbers Family Farm, on sustainable produce and heritage meats, all raised within a dozen miles of the farm. West Michigan is a major hub of sustainable farmers with many working hard to keep it that way. Touring farms is now known as agri-tourism. At the farm dinner, hosted by the farm family, Slow Food West Michigan Potawatomi and Tilling-to-Table, it feels like I'm a thousand miles away from Grand Rapids. And in

a way, I am. Out here, three long tables stretched a good distance seating a goat cheese-maker, asparagus broker, restaurateurs, Community Supported Agriculture farmers, and enthusiast eaters. The Tilling-to-Table tastemakers whip up delicious dishes starting with an amuse bouche of celery and mushroom phyllo pouch with a blueberry balsamic reduction and melon and cucumber gazpacho topped with a basil mint creme fraiche. We move onto the arugula and mustard greens salad with beets, red onion, cilantro and goat cheese tossed with apple cider-honey vinaigrette, followed by grilled trout draped over a polenta cake and tomato ragu. The herb crusted pork tenderloin topping red pepper cassoulet, sparkling raspberry sorbet intermezzo and peach cobbler with ginger ice cream pushed the boundaries of what farmstead cooking can taste and look like. Everything is produced on the farm (in a tent!) by the culinary students from the Secchica Institute for Culinary Education at Grand Rapids Community College. The students founded the Tilling to Table (open to all, including non-students) to engage the community in sustainable farming practices. They grow food on a plot of land at GRCC's McCabe-Marlowe house, and maintain an herb garden in the Green Roof of the college's Applied Technology Center. At every turn, there's a food story waiting to be shared.

Karen Lubbers became the center of the crowd, her story fascinating. She hasn't been to a grocery store in years, perhaps she ran in once or twice to buy Saran Wrap. Her family grows all the food they consume, she's partial to raising heritage pigs for their farm table, milking Jersey cows for their gallons of raw milk, and planting heirloom seeds because they are open-pollinated. That means, you can save the seeds in the fall and plant them again in the spring and you will get the same crop. "You can't do that with a hybrid which is a cross, so you don't know what you are going to get. I like Seed Savers dedicated to preserving seeds that are becoming extinct." For the Slow Food Potawatomi convivium, the Lubbers grow heirloom seedlings from U.S. Ark of Taste, a catalog of more than 900 delicious foods in danger of extinction. By growing Ark products we help ensure they remain in production and on our plates. The seedlings, including red fig tomatoes, Aunt Ruby's German green tomatos, New Mexico basil, Crane melon and Amish pie pumpkin, to name just a few—are available at their farm for $3 a pot.

Each one carries an interesting backstory, like the red fig tomatoes. "In the old days people used to dry the tomato shaped like a small pear and then pack them into crates and store in their basements," she began. "They were called figs because when they dried, they got sweet and you could use them as a fig." This is way before the whole sun-dried tomato craze. As we walk the field, Karen Lubbers points out German pink and German green heirloom tomatoes. "That's heirloom corn and it gets 10 feet or more high and it tastes like corn instead of sweetness, although it is sweet. This year, I planted country gentlemen and stole evergreen, don't you love it, along with the kind of root vegetables —turnips, rutabagas, parsnips— people have gotten out of the habit of preparing."

"The whole family makes a living on the land. It has its challenging, but it has worked so well." Karen says.

Six or seven years ago, Lubbers son, Casey, started an organic bakery, Little Red Rooster, from the farmstead, located steps away from the milk house. He has many accounts with independent grocery stores, West Michigan co-op, D&W Fresh Markets and Fulton Street Farmers Market. "It's kind of amazing how it all happened," says Casey Lubbers, who went out West, attended the San Francisco Baking Institute, and returned to his family's farm to start a bakery. With King's Milling flour in Lowell, Casey Lubbers kneads together sandwich bread, hamburger and hot dog buns and dinner rolls. "Right now I'm so busy. Sometime I don't know if I'm coming or going."

See, more and more people seek wholesome, sustainable, foods for their table, but underneath there's something even bigger. "There is yearning for connection and authenticity and historically food has represented that," Karen says. "People are gathering their food and that can be frustrating. Have to go here to get raw milk, there to get pasture-raised beef, there for farmstead cheese."

It's all enough to make you feel like a modern-day hunter-gatherer because you're hunting all over town, county, perhaps the state, for high-quality sustainable raised ingredients—real, whole foods. It shouldn't be that hard.

Good from the goat

Barbara Jenness, of Dancing Goat Creamery in Byron Center, wins you right over when she cheerily steps out of her 100-year-old barn. With long silver braids swinging and her herd of American Alpine goats nipping at her heels, Barbara is a cheese evangelist. Her onsite cheese plant may be one of the smallest in the state, but she talks of it fondly, with a wonderful gleam in her eyes, while conducting cheese workshops all over the state. Barbara has taught hundreds of Michiganders and others to make small-scale, high-quality cheese. She also joins Dr. John Partridge and Bill Robb on an instructional team of the MSU Artisanal Hands-On Cheese Making Workshop at the university-run dairy plant.

When visiting Barbara, just hope she invites you into the kitchen for one of her signature breakfast cookies with a special ingredient from her line of work. The amazing treats are made of oatmeal, nuts, coconuts, cornflakes, dried cherries, chocolate chips, and her own farmstead whey in place of buttermilk.

How did she get into the cheese business? Barbara had built a herd of American Alpine goats to produce and sell a line of goat-milk soap, studded with flower petals, rosemary, cranberry seeds, and comfrey root. With all that goat milk around, she decided to make plain chevre (French for fresh goat milk cheese) to keeps things from going to waste. After workshops in Montreal, at Pure Luck Goat Farm in Texas, and at North Carolina State University, she was certified as a master cheese maker through the Vermont Institute of Artisan Cheese.

"When I first started making cheese, I was so excited that I made a different cheese every day," Barbara recalls. "They were all terrible, because you don't figure out the nuances of it. If you're going to make

cheese, make one—and make it good. Then add your second cheese. For years, I have done chevre … so now I'm adding other mold-ripened cheese."

At her small working dairy farm, mama goats, six kids, and a lone male named Little Richard, prance around, head-butt, graze, and gallop around a paddock leading to the rambling farmhouse. On a June summer morning, Barbara and her high school helper work with the goat milk in various stages of production: pasteur-

izing in one unit, curdling in cheesecloth bags over a metal rack, and cooling the chevre in giant plastic tubs. This is farmstead cheese in the making; that is the term for an enterprise that harvests product from its own animals and performs every step of the process on-site. As soon as the cheese is ready, Barbara also does the deliveries to her customer stores and restaurants.

Besides Barbara's silver-medal status with the American Cheese Society, her Dancing Goat chevre was

featured during the Slow Food Nation four-day craft-food exhibition in San Francisco. Her son, Jason Moniz, who is a chef in that city, often features Barbara's product on the menu. Barbara and two other Michigan farmers served as Michigan State University delegates to another Slow Food exhibition in Turin, Italy. This is a second career of sorts for Barbara, who also has a veterinary technology degree from Pierce College in Los Angeles, and associate's degree from Windward Community College in Hawaii, and a bachelor's degree in biology from Grand Valley State University.

Back at her farm, Barbara makes nearly 150 to 175 pounds of goat cheese a week. Currently, besides the chevre, Dancing Goat's lineup includes cracked black pepper cheese, red pepper, sun-dried tomato, honey-orange zest, Michigan cherry pecan chevre log, and feta marinated in sun-dried tomatoes and olive oil. A new favorite is pesto chevre, made with basil and garlic from Barbara's garden.

"If you have ever tasted goat's cheese that has tasted really goaty, that's not very good. That's because goat's milk is real susceptible to poor handling," she says. "So if it is made commercially, it gets pumped into a tank where it's held for several days. Then it gets pumped into a truck, sloshing all the way to the plant,

where it is pumped into a vat. All those things break down that milk."

In Barbara's farmstead operation, within 15 minutes of milking, it's tanked and is always hand-carried in buckets. "We don't pump it. It never gets pumped in any way, and it's strained twice," she says.

When the milk is prepared into the makings for cheese and needs aging, each container has a lot number on it for tracing. When the cheese is ready for release, off it goes to independent stores, restaurants, and food co-ops in Kent, Allegan, Ottawa, and Muskegon counties.

Great taste in Suttons Bay

While John and Anne Hoyt of Leelanau Cheese Co., in Suttons Bay, gently heat fresh cow's milk from nearby Garvin Farm, you can watch the procedure from a wall-size, plate-glass viewing window at the Black Star Farms tasting room. Everything is spotlessly clean here, and the milk that was fresh just that morning is creamy white as it warms in a huge stainless steel kettle. It's an early step in the making of another delectable round of Leelanau cheese.

The company's artisan cheese named Raclette is ideal for melting in fondues, and is the pride and joy of the business. Another aged product from Leelanau beat out more than 1,200 entries to take best-of-show at the 24th annual American Cheese Society competition. The cheese-makers always use vegetable rennet to coagulate the milk, and no colors or preservatives are added. Wheels of Raclette, weighing 8 to 10 pounds each, are about three inches thick, with a golden rind typical of the Swiss and French washed-rind cheeses brushed with

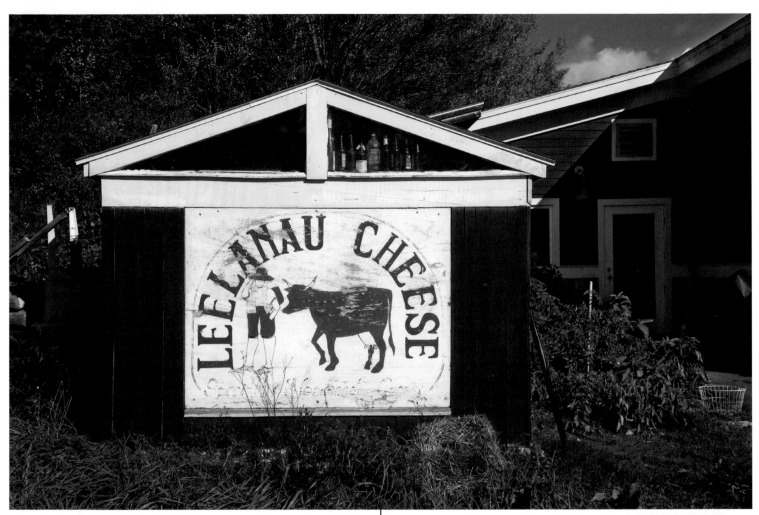

saltwater brine. The mild Raclette cures in about three to four months, while the harder, aged Raclette takes eight to 10 months.

John and Anne know a thing or two about this special food craft. After all, they had a history with cheese-making dating back to their younger days visiting the Swiss Alps village of Eison. John learned cheese-making in Europe, where he studied at the Chateauneuf School of Agriculture in the Valais region of Switzerland renowned for fine cheese.

One day, John recalls, while working in the Alpine village of Eison, the French-born Anne and two friends came ambling up the mountain. "And here comes my (future) wife, walking up with a couple of friends with their bags on a pony. They ended up staying with us. She learned how to milk cows and cooked us good meals because we were eating rice and lentils every day. She's French and knows how to cook." Together, they worked as cheese-makers for several alpine farm cooperatives where the cows graze the vast mountain pastures, in Thyon and Veysonnaz, and the cheese is set up for the day after each milking. After nine years there, John brought Anne to Michigan. He eventually earned a degree in French from Eastern University, and the couple moved to the beautiful Leelanau Peninsula.

"When I was a kid, I used to travel up here, all around northern Michigan and the Upper Peninsula, with my father, who liked to fish," John says. "So when we returned, I would bring my wife up here and, driving around it felt a little like Bordeaux; all these cherry trees and just a few vineyards at the time."

First, the pair found menial jobs—medicinal gardening and pruning vineyards—just to keep from going broke. Then a friend purchased a stainless kettle in a salvage yard for $100, which was great, considering that big of a pot would retail for thousands of dollars brand new, John says. Next, John revamped an old space near Leelanau Cellars' tasting room. "I got that little kettle going, and we created Leelanau Cheese Co. out of it," John recalls. "We would make eight wheels —about 60 to 70 pounds of cheese—every other day, and we just built the business with that. This is really the ultimate in hand-crafting, because it's a lot of work. We are far from industrial (size and) can only make so much in that kettle. We try to make it happen as much as we can."

Five years later, Leelanau Cheese Co. expanded by relocating into Black Star Farms' tasting room, and the business grew exponentially, earning award after award for its products. In an L-shaped underground aging vault at the business, the cheeses age a minimum of three months. In the facility, equipped with

Switzerland's finest machinery, every batch of Raclette is created, washed in a brine bath, and parked on an ash board to call home for three months or more.

John and Anne tend to the cheese daily, turning and brushing the many wheels with a brine solution to encourage the aging into a rich orange hue and distinctive, unforgettable flavor.

"It was a lot of hard work, broken backs. But not failed cheese."

"We struggled a lot," John reflects on the long process of making the business. "It was a lot of hard work, broken backs. But not failed cheese. I haven't ruined a batch yet."

The Hoyts also make a popular flavored Fromage Blanc, which is a hand-blended spread that comes in plain herb, garlic and herb, and peppercorn and herb. All are excellent as appetizers, on sandwiches, baked potatoes, or tangled with hot pasta. A cherry fromage blanc, both tart and sweet, is divine on bagels.

Farm Country Cheese

In the midstate town of Lakeview, the Amish of Montcalm County know plenty about making old-fashioned cheese, having worked in the craft for more than 25 years. At the Farm Country Cheese Store in Lakeview, the area's Amish farmers bring their milk in old-style 80-pound cans to a cheese plant built there in 1984.

"We do mostly everything the old-fashioned way," says Dan Miller, who works at the plant his father helped build. "We get between 600 to 700 of those 80-pound cans every day. We buy our milk from 112 Amish farms nearby. Most of these farmers have as few as two cows, and some as many as 20. It's all hand-milked, every drip of milk is hand squeezed from the cows. We're not mechanized at all."

When cows roam to feed, grazing on carotene-rich pasture, and are given plenty of fresh air and sunlight, they produce milk that is full of wholesome goodness. At the cheese plant, the Amish test the Holstein and Jersey milk for bacteria and antibiotics, then pasteurize it before it's poured into one of the old English-style open vats in the cheese-making room. The largest vat holds 20,000 pounds of milk, which becomes 2,000 pounds of cheese; the other two vats each hold about 12,000 pounds of milk.

"Our boss takes tremendous pride in the fact we only pump our milk twice. It's been proven over and over that the more you pump the milk before you make it into cheese, the more you break down the enzymes," Dan says. "We believe we have one of the healthiest cheeses out there. It is all whole milk—we haven't separated the cream or anything like that."

They produce old-fashioned table cheese in 10-pound blocks with whole ingredients, not fake flavoring or powders. The cheese is unreal with freshness and flavor — studded with real cooked and crumbled bacon, habanero peppers, freshly ground horseradish, fennel, caraway, dill, just to name a few of the special blends.

In 2006, when Jim and Judy Nunley purchased the cheese plant, the couple sought to find a more dependable retail market for the cheese. They soon put together an impressive distribution network, including locations in Grand Rapids, Cadillac, and Traverse City.

"I think more and more people appreciate a good, wholesome cheese that is as close to organic as you can get," Dan says. "We are about as organic as you can get without certification. Most of our farmers are so small that, to spend thousands of dollars to be certified organic, is just out of their reach. We try to treat the animals as we would treat ourselves. The less chemical, the better."

Old-fashioned Cream-line Bottles

Here are four of the state's micro-dairies selling cream-line milk in glass jars:

Calder Dairy: 1020 Southfield Road, Lincoln Park, MI 48146, (313) 381-8858. The dairy store is open 7 a.m. to 10 p.m. and the ice cream parlor is open from noon to 9 p.m. daily. Calder Diary is the granddaddy of the micro-creameries.

Cream Cup Dairy: 7377 Feldhak Road, Kaleva, MI 49645, (231) 889-4158. In 2005, David Miller figured he had to go big or micro-small because paying someone to haul the milk away was eating away the bottom line. For several years, he shipped milk as a bulk commodity, but began to bottle and sell on his own almost five years ago. "People tell me they like the taste of the milk because it's full of cream," David says. He attributes that to his slow vat pasteurization in which the milk is heated in a vat (or tank) to 145 degrees retaining the organisms that grow slowly and produce spores the good stuff that can be obliterated with ultra pasteurization. Dave milks just 12 cows, bottling the old-fashioned cream line (full-fat) milk into glass jars available at the farm and independent retail markets in Ludington, Manistee and Benzonia.

Hilhof Dairy, Organic Dairy Products: 468 160th Avenue, Hersey, MI 49639, (231) 832-1313; HilhofDairy.com. Farm store open from noon to 5 p.m. Monday through Wednesday and Friday through Sunday. Hilhof Dairy's Connie Straathof said, "We're doing milk the old-fashioned way. We try to make it as pure as we can. It's all non-homogenized (which) means you can digest it easier.

Shetler's Dairy Farm: 5436 Tyler Rd. SE, Kalaska, MI, 49646, (231) 258-8216. Farm store open 11 a.m. to 6 p.m. Monday through Saturday. "There's a world of difference in our glass-bottled, farm-fresh milk," says Sally Shetler of Shetler's Dairy Farm.

Amish Cheese: Farm Country Cheese House: 7263 Kendaville Road, Lakeview, MI 48850, farmcountry-cheese.com, The retail store is open 9 a.m. to 5 p.m., Monday through Saturday. To watch cheese-making in progress, visit from 9 a.m. to 2 p.m. Monday through Friday. For group tours, contact (989) 352-7779.

Producers in the Michigan Cheese Makers Cooperative:

Cowslip Creamery: 826 Luce Ave. SW, Grand Rapids, MI 49534, (616) 726-2462, cowslipcreamery.com

Dancing Goat Creamery: 10385 Wilson Ave. SW, Byron Center, MI 49315, (616) 878-7961, dogwoodfarm.net

Evergreen Lane Farm and Creamery: 1824 68th St., Fennville, MI 49408, (269) 543-9900, evergreenlanefarm.com

Four Corners Creamery: 102 East Chicago Blvd., Tecumseh, MI 49286, (517) 423-6000, boulevardmarket.com

Grassfields Cheese: 14238 60th Ave., Coopersville, MI 49404, (616) 997-8251, grassfieldscheese.com

Greenbush Farms: 8003 N. Scott Road, St. Johns, MI 48879, (989) 224-3432, greenbush-farms.com

Greystone Farm and Creamery: 14325 Jerusalem Road, Chelsea, MI 48118, (734) 475-9560, greystonefarmandcreamery.com

Leelanau Cheese Company: 10844 E. Revold Road Suttons Bay, MI 49682, (231) 271-2600, Leelanaucheese.com

Mattawan Artisan Creamery: 22884 44th Ave., Mattawan, MI 49071, (269) 668-4218, kalcarbon.com Michigan State University Dairy: Farm Lane, East Lansing, MI 48824, (517) 355-7713 ext. 179

Zingerman's Creamery: 3723 Plaza Drive, Ann Arbor, MI 48108 (734) 929-0500, zingermanscreamery.com

FROM THE BARNYARD

As we take in the rural scene, out on the country lanes and open fields, we meet Michigan's hands-on, sustainable-agriculture herdspeople. They care about their footprint in the world. Or, more precisely, that the animals they raise get to make some footprints outdoors. A key part of humanely raising livestock and other barnyard animals is to let them have a life on the land, not a caged nightmare of an existence. These farmers understand the balance of sun, soil, and water rather than relying on antibiotics, steroids, and growth-promoting hormones.

This small but growing movement toward pasture-raised products is a welcome trend. Consumer demand is growing for meats that are produced small in scale and high in quality rather than mass-produced and shrink-wrapped.

Old Pine Farm in Manchester and Gallagher Centennial Farm in Grand Traverse County are good examples of the smaller operations taking root and supplying stores with a real alternative to the mega-feedlot supply chain. And the customer base is finally there. Consumers are showing they want to buy directly from a local farmer who raises animals the old-fashioned way, on grassy pastureland.

"They want to come here and see what's going on," Joanne Gallagher says of a certain segment of today's consumers. "They want to buy directly from us because we have accountability. They know where to find us."

"In the stores," she says, "the beef—nearly all of it—comes from a feed lot. Nothing comes from an individual farmer."

"They want to buy directly from us because we have accountability."

Crane Dance Farm in Middleville is another good example, where even the breeding is left up to Mother Nature rather than artificial insemination. When

"the new old way."

tending pastures, mending fences, and, of course, daily feeding and mucking. Besides all that and the maintenance of farm buildings and equipment, these entrepreneurs also market and directly sell their meat, eggs, and other goods.

As more consumers focus on eating locally and healthy, it's not just about the veggies and fruit; one's protein-source choices are part of the equation, too. This is not just about carnivores/ominvores, either, but for anybody who looks to barnyard food sources in their diet, such as vegetarians who love their eggs or the many who eat a wide range of foods but not red meat. So-called niche foods are really catching on in the marketplace: free-range chickens, "heritage" turkeys, farm-raised eggs, and even bison meat—a tasty, wild choice increasingly available in the market. The North American native buffalo has been part of the landscape for millennia, so you can't get any more local than that.

the time is right, Crane Dance simply puts bull and cow together and lets nature takes it course. Later, the newborns are left under their mothers' care to grow peacefully into yearlings, nursing and grazing all the way until they wean naturally. Instead of chemical-laden feeds, these animals eat the real thing —grasses and plants in the pasture —renewable resources when they are properly managed by the property owner.

By contrast, industrial animal farms have done away with pasture-based practices in favor of a confined-space upbringing. No more fattening up on pasture grass, nosing about on the land, or lazing away under the Michigan sky.

Yes, it usually costs more to do it this way, to let animals gain their poundage at a natural pace. There's more labor to it, more hands-on involvement. Small-farm operators work long days

In some ways, livestock loose in the pasture and barnyard is the "new old way," says Bill Robb, a Michigan State University senior Cooperative Extension Service educator. Tried and true livestock-management

practices are returning. More farms are putting their animals out to green pastures and letting chickens loose to peck for something edible. Putting up your own beef in the freezer is all the rage, and city dwellers even are raising chickens out back.

"All of these factors drive the niche farming market," says Bill Robb, who grew up on a family farm in Fowlerville, so he knows quite a bit about former practices on a typical small farm.

Years ago, more beef farmers ran cow-calf pairs in which the farmer would breed a cow and help care for her one or two offsprings. When the calf is weaned and reaches maturity, it is sold, usually to family or a friend. Back in the day, when small USDA slaughter and packing houses dotted the countryside, people went down the road, had the animal processed, and put up most of it in the freezer. Much of that practice went away in recent decades, when federal rule changes made it harder for small farms to stay in the game.

Hog heaven in Middleville

Outside Middleville, south of Grand Rapids, Mr. Tambourine Man, aka Tambo, a red-colored Tamworth boar, is in hog heaven. Tambo is rooting like crazy through pasture grass, looking for something tasty to eat. This field is full of purslane, curly dock, pigweed, Pennsylvania smartweed, white clover, red clover, orchard grass, Queen Anne's lace, and much more. Many of these plants are labeled weeds by conventional farmers and blasted with herbicides.

Not around here; not at Crane Dance Farms. In fact, owners Jill Johnson and Mary Wills welcome the ecological diversity, knowing that it ultimately helps to foster soil health and support all kinds of life above ground, including Tambo and the local birds, bees, butterflies, and people. "The animals will go right to that flower because there's something in there that they need, that they want," says Jill, whose Crane Dance Farm is Michigan's first Animal Cruelty Approved pig farm.

"Animals in confinement are going to be agitated."

This Tamworth boar—a "heritage" pig—is part of a happy, healthy family that he's personally responsible for expanding. The pastured sows at Crane Dance are wonderful rare breeds that can be hard to find, such as Berkshire pigs originating from Britain; crossbred pigs from heritage stock including Mulefoot hogs, with one-toed hooves like a mule; Red Wattle, a massive, red hog with a fleshy wattle on each side of the neck; and Choctaw, a domestic pig favored by Native Americans.

Here, all the animals roam free from birthday to

market day. They don't really ask for much, anyway: a safe place to sleep, a chance to nurse their young, time to poke about the pasture, and something good to eat. Here's what doesn't happen to the pigs here. Their noses aren't pierced multiple times with rings to painfully stop them from rooting, their ears aren't clipped, and their tails aren't docked (cut off with a knife or shears).

In modern, industrial agriculture, pigs live not on farms but in confinement structures called concentrated animal feeding operations (CAFOs.) They are housed in hulking, steel warehouses, inside small cells without access to fresh air or stimulation—eating, sleeping, eliminating all in the same pen. No wonder they become agitated and look for a fight. When a pig is confined in a metal cage, never to see the light of day, it can go crazy and start fighting with its own kind, its community.

"Animals in confinement are going to be agitated, angry and will attack each other, especially if their nutritional needs aren't being met," says Jill, who has degrees from Western Michigan University and Albion College.

"People say you can't have pigs and poultry near each other. Well, we've had a mama pig baby-sit a duck on her nest and block her in, protecting her so nobody could get to her babies. They are not eating (the ducks or

eggs) because they don't need to. Even our cranky sow, Lucky, doesn't mind turkey poults wandering around in her area."

At Crane Dance, the rugged outdoor hogs produce meat with exceptional color, flavor and texture. When the pigs are market-ready, they are taken to a small custom packer nearby. They produce a nitrate-free line of hickory-smoked meats, including bacon and ham. Nothing infused under pressure with liquid chemical smoke; it's the real thing. Delicious, clean spices are used to make their sausage, which is free of preservatives, flavor enhancers, and MSG. They grind shoulder and leg meat into their sausage so that it's leaner and tastier.

On a visit to Crane Dance, we stroll outside toward a cluster of cows, a mix of shaggy Scottish Highlands, Black Angus-Simmental crosses, caramel-colored Jerseys, and Charolais cows. Jill and Mary call

out to the animals by name. They seem relaxed and not at all concerned about the visit.

"These animals are so social that you can get right in the pasture with them," Jill says. "They have real personalities because we nurture that. They are born here, they nurse here, and they run all around here. From birth to market day, we try to do right by them."

They are big believers in rotating the animals from pasture to pasture, which keeps the soil healthy. That method is called controlled grazing. Here's how it works: The cattle eat and trample the grass, then are followed by the flock of egg-laying chickens. The chickens have nighttime houses called egg-mobiles that move with them to each pasture assignment. During the day, they strut through the field, spreading the cow patties (nature's fertilizer when managed properly.)

This is a hard-working posse of chickens. More than 40 heirloom breeds peck and run around the field. There is the French meat breed called Freedom Rangers, and there are Cornish crosses, Buff Polish chicken, Araucanas and many others. "They all have a purpose in addition to lay-

ing eggs," Jill says. "Having chicken follow the cows is a really good thing. As they spread the manure around, they eat the bugs that are cow parasites. Their job is to fertilize and sanitize the pasture for the cows."

In addition to pigs and cows, Crane Dance Farm raises heritage sheep and poultry (including chickens, geese, guinea, ducks, and turkeys) on open pasture.

Most of Crane Dance's ruminants and pigs are bred and birthed right on the farm, assuring a good life from beginning to end.

Because Crane Dance Farm does such an exceptional job of protecting the animals and environment, the Animal Welfare Approved organization rewarded Jill and Mary with an expense-paid trip to Willie Nelson's 25th anniversary Farm Aid concert in Milwaukee. At 2010's Farm Aid 25: Growing Hope for America, Crane Dance joined two other Animal Welfare Approved farms at the event's Animal Cruelty Approved booth.

"That is our payola," says Jill, who sells from market booths in Ada, Grand Rapids, and Holland. "We're not getting rich off this. If we had to do this and throw them on a truck and get a check in the mail, there would be no joy in that. We want relationships with people. We want to know their food experience. We want to hear how they used particular cuts of meat. We want to see the joy on their faces when they tell us how absolutely wonderful that it is."

Walking back from the field on a visit, Jill shares the origin of the farm's name. "Our farm is Crane Dance because, when I originally bought the farm, the sandhill cranes flew in here in the spring," Jill says. "It was a reminder for me to remember that, whatever I did here, I didn't want to interrupt the cranes. I later learned in Eastern philosophy that the dance of the cranes represents the joy of life. We want to make sure our animals have that. It might be a short life, but while they are here, they will get to express themselves the way nature intended."

Living on the land

Kristen Hirth, at Old Pine Farm in Manchester, south of Ann Arbor, also believes in pastured-raised animal husbandry. The animals live outdoors on the finest ingredients: grass, certified-organic feed, sunshine, clean water—the way nature intended.

"We use organic methods (and are) trying to obtain a pasture-based certification, so it's all about humane farming," says Kris, who runs the farm with her sons, Josh and Casey. In October 2010, 18-year-old Casey, a college student, was the youngest Terra Madre delegate representing Slow Food Huron Valley. Terra Madre is a natural foods and farming symposium in Italy where more than 5,000 people gather to promote sustainable local food production in harmony with the environment and to share knowledge on the subject.

and blended with everything else on the farm, meaning the cows co-exist with the chickens and so on. All of this outdoor living reduces stress on the population, she says, and certainly in comparison with being crammed into an industrial farming facility. The result of their care is a grass-fed beef deliciously marbled with all that outdoor-living goodness, and it is sold by beef quarters or through the CSA memberships. Instead of a weekly box of Swiss chard and garlic from your friendly local farmer, the Old Pine members pick up monthly boxes of professionally butchered and wrapped meats.

In the meat CSA, the participants pay according to the share size they select. Based on the current membership, Kris sets about raising a certain number of animals to meet the monthly share requirements. The popular subscription boxes (Old Pine has a waiting list, Kris says) can include extras such as freshly processed guinea pork in September, heritage turkey in November, and a duck or goose for December.

Those extras can take a lot of work, but variety is key to what the local-food movement has to offer over the supermarket. A look at the Old Pine Farm menagerie is a case in point. Shaggy Scottish Highlanders, Texas longhorns, Shorthorns, and Belted Galloways

The workshops were "inspiring and useful," says Casey, a culinary arts major, who still works on Old Pine Farm. On the weekends, he continues to throw chicken feed, help raise the grass-fed beef and corral the free-range hogs as needed. Josh handles the heavy work on the farm. From hay production and hauling to moving cattle from pasture to pasture, he is in the thick of it.

The Hirth family makes sure their cattle never see a feedlot, stand in their own waste, or eat chemically enhanced feed. Old Pine Farm, in fact, is a unique operation in the state, as it runs Michigan's only meat CSA (community supported agriculture) program. Local people pay an annual fee to become a member of the farm and receive regular shares of the meat products generated there. The Hirths' pasture-based hoof stock and poultry—cows, pigs, sheep, goats, chickens, and emu—are humanely raised on grass, organic feed, and chemical-free hay grown by the family.

It's important to Kris that her animals live a good life from start to finish. Most are pasture-raised

"They don't do much but eat grass."

graze two pastures the Hirth family operates, one of 50 acres southwest of Jackson and the other of 15 acres about five miles from that site. In these fenced pastures, Hirth also raises Navajo Churros and Tunis, the country's oldest sheep breeds. "They don't do much but eat grass," says Kris, "but they help keep the land healthy by working the soil with their feet."

In the spring, hogs move onto the pasture and stay awhile, roaming there into the summer. "I like the rare breeds, like the guinea hogs, also called guinea forest hogs," Kris says. "There are only about 600 left in the country. They're hearty hogs and terrific foragers—and their fat is wonderful and different. The down side is they are only half the size of the standard-size hog, so they are a CSA specialty item because they don't provide much meat."

The guinea hogs are kept separate from the other breeds because they aren't allowed corn in their diet. They put on plenty of fat naturally and would become unhealthy if they also ate corn, Kris says. The rest of the Old Pine hogs get a certified-organic corn mix, but the guineas are fed a special blend of oats, veggies and more.

"These animals on-pasture really enrich the soil. Plus, broad genetic diversity is a good thing. Heritage breeds are adapted to live outdoors on-pasture, sleeping in the barn, foraging; and they can breed all by themselves," she says.

Enterprising Gallagher Family

Joanne and Douglas Gallagher are practical people trying to stay in a business others have had to leave. The Gallaghers are centennial farmers (established 1905) managing dairy cows, cattle, and cherry orchards. Joanne, who also works in photography and prints a line of notecards featuring her work, grew up on the nearby Old Mission Peninsula and has raised a few farmers in

the next generation. Daughter Pennie (Gallagher) Halpin works the Land of Goshen sustainable farm with her husband, Chris, and their large family. On 30 acres near the town of Kaleva, Pennie and Chris diversified to keep their farm afloat, running a CSA venture, a goat dairy with micro-creamery, a meat-processing service, and a farm-fresh eggs outlet with 100 laying hens. Land of Goshen products are used and sold at several restaurants and stores, including Trattoria Stella and the Oryana Natural Foods Market in Traverse City.

Like her daughter and son-in-law, Joanne had been looking for a way to keep on farming, especially in an environmentally sustainable way, and Anthony helped develop a formula for the family.

"Our son wanted something different to help

sustain the dairy operation, because it is a lot of work and milk prices aren't anything," Joanne says. "They go up and down and have for a while. We ended up buying 37 young heifers from a guy we know. We got them bred and started raising our herd. So all the cattle are born and raised on the farm. We raise the heifers for their milk and the steers, Holsteins and Black Angus, for their meat. The Holstein is excellent, but it's leaner; the Black Angus has more fat, more flavor. They are pastured and fed our own, old-fashioned corn. We don't give them genetically modified corn."

Today, many consumers want to buy quarters, halves, or more of pastured beef neatly packaged and frozen as roasts, steaks, and ground. It's a multitude of factors leading to this market niche: people want to avoid product from mega-feed-lots, they want to support local farms, they want animals to be raised humanely, and are looking to eat healthier. By law, the Gallaghers must send their animals to a slaughterhouse inspected by the U.S. Department of Agriculture, so they use two licensed northern Michigan slaughterhouses: L&J Meat Market in Lake City, and Ebels Family Center in Falmouth. The Gallaghers' meats are aged, cut, wrapped, and frozen for easy handling, and the product line includes sausages, bolognas, brats, bacons, and hams without nitrates.

The Gallaghers have found a public hungry for a food line that comes from the local community, and because the family business uses a certified slaughterhouse, farmers markets are an attractive marketing outlet. Three years ago, the

Gallaghers ramped up their presence in the area with Anthony and his wife, Katie, leading the efforts. They now are fixtures at the farmers markets in Traverse City, Alberta, Elk Rapids, and Frankfort.

"That is why I was taking a nap when you came," Joanne says to her Culinary Roadtrip visitors. "I've got to get up at 5 a.m. to get the samples made, (then) leave at a quarter after 6 to go to Frankfort. It's a lot of work. My husband milks those cows twice a day at 6:30. We don't take vacations."

A lot of work, always, but the rewards are beginning to show, too.

Buffalo comes of age again

The bison herd that travelers can view along U.S. 37, south of Traverse City, is fascinating. At first glance, from a distance, they look like any old cattle grazing the pasture. Get a little closer, though, and it's something else. The large shaggy beasts, with their humped backs, are unique and all-American.

A little more than a century ago, of course, bison numbers plummeted to an estimated 500 head across the continent—from an incredible 30 million peak decades earlier. Big-game hunters, westward expansion, and

railroad construction nearly took the buffalo out of buffalo country, according to a rancher's handbook of the National Buffalo Association.

On that Traverse City pasture motorists can view the herd that Brad Oleson's late grandfather, Gerald, started in 1954. He bought 20 head out West and trucked them back to help market his Oleson Markets in the area. Brad and his brother, Don, now run the family business, with Brad managing the herd and his brother overseeing the stores. Brad says the buffalo herd is down to 400 these days, from an all-time high of 1,000.

"At one point, we had the largest herd east of the Mississippi," Brad says. For a time, things slacked off when people seemed to lose

"At one point, we had the largest herd east of the Mississippi."

their interest in buffalo meat, he says, but times have changed again. The Oleson brothers are looking to breed the herd back up to 600 or so at their two locations. Their larger pasture is the one along Kyselka Road, plus they keep a tiny herd adjacent to the water-park resort south of Traverse City, along U.S. 31.

"The demand is growing exponentially in the last two years," Brad says. "It has caught me off-guard, personally. People weren't educated on it. As more people get more health-conscious, though, and find out how pure and natural the meat is, the demand increases."

Bison meat is lean and nutrition-packed, particularly compared with grain-fattened domestic animals from big feedlots. Of the two North American subspecies, Canadian and Great Plains, Brad raises the former. The Great Plains buffalo has a longer beard, shorter legs, and a bigger hump. The Canadian, also called Great Woods, has longer legs for easier walking in the snow, a furrier crown, and square hump. The Oleson animals are raised on-pasture, with no growth hormones and/or chemicals; in the winter, they are fed a little hay. They live on the farm from birth to market day. The appeal of bison meat, all natural from ranch to dinner plate, is growing swiftly in the local-food movement, and the Olesons are doing a brisk mail-order business plus a lot of sales to independently owned northern Michigan restaurants. Brad and Don, along with some cousins, own two stores in Traverse City and one each in Manistee, Charlevoix, and Petoskey. Buffalo steaks, roasts, ground, and hot dogs—fresh and frozen—are sold there.

The nutritional numbers for buffalo are pretty impressive. The meat has less fat, cholesterol, and calories per serving than beef, pork, or chicken. A 100-gram portion of cooked buffalo meat has 143 calories, compared with beef's 211, pork's 212 calories, and skinless chicken's 190. Of commonly available meats in the marketplace, it is considered the healthiest, the Olesons say. In terms of fat, the numbers are equally low; a 10-gram piece of buffalo meat has 2.42 grams of fat, while beef has 9.28 and skinless chicken has 7.4. Bison meat even packs a higher amount of iron and protein than Atlantic salmon.

Bison meat is a little more expensive than cattle beef because supply still is low compared to the rising demand. The price also reflects the longer time it takes to raise a buffalo to maturity. When you raise cattle from birth to market, it takes about a year and a half, but bison doesn't mature until about a year later, so the price reflects that additional rearing time.

Contrary to popular belief, bison are not slow-witted, prodding animals, despite their shaggy, lumbering appearance, Brad says. Spend a little time with them, and their social personalities emerge. "Buffalo are extremely family-oriented," Brad says. "They absolutely need other animals to live, to sustain. They are extremely protective of each other. If one is hurt, the whole herd will take care of it, surround it, and protect it from predators."

The local radio guys in Traverse City like to say the bisons' behavior is a weather barometer in those parts, Brad says. When severe weather threatens, like a blizzard, the bison huddle, congregating together in the valley. In nice weather, they sprawl far apart on the hilltops.

They are a pretty self-sustaining creature, Brad says, but bison do like to roam, so he spends a lot of time checking fences. Brad also has learned that you don't want to make a bison cranky. The herbivores stand up to 6 feet tall and can weigh a ton.

"One thing you learn early on is you can't push them around, literally," he says. "If push comes to shove, they will even take on a big black bear. A black bear might think he's the biggest, baddest dude in the wild, but a buffalo won't back down, and that bear will turn and run."

For bison (buffalo) nearest you, check out Michigan Bison Association website michiganbison.com; click on the membership list to find locations. Also try National Bison Association bisoncentral.com; search the buyer's guide page by typing in state and/or request bison meat, tours, hunts, hides, other byproducts.

Eatwild.com lists 800 U.S. ranches and farms selling pasture-raised meats directly to customers. Michigan link: eatwild.com/products/michigan. Also, state-by-state Beyond the Farm section sources buying clubs, stores, restaurants selling grass-fed meats; for Michigan-specific, eatwild.com/products/michiganresources.

Local Harvest at localharvest.org links to thousands of small and organic food producers, including meat and poultry operations. Searchable by map or product sought.

Michigan Land Institute's Taste the Local Difference at LocalDifference.org, details 160 farms and the products they sell in northwest Michigan; pocket-size guides available by calling (231) 941-6584.

Crane Dance Farm: Middleville MI 49333; (616) 293-1091; cranedancefarm.com

Old Pine Farm: Manchester MI 48158; oldpinefarm.biz

Gallagher's Centennial Farm: 5891 N. Long Lake Road, Traverse City MI 49684; (231) 421-5199, (231) 218-0771; gallagherfarms.com

Oleson's Food Stores in Traverse City, Petoskey, Charlevoix, and Manistee; olesonsfoods.com

"Everything, except the vintage candy collection and real cane cola soda, is all Michigan," says owner Andrew Milaukas. "All the produce comes from farmers within 30 miles, and we are very proud of that."

Andrew doesn't have farming roots, but he does have an eye for beauty, aesthetics, and adventure. After graduating from the renowned Savannah (Ga.) College of Art and Design, he jokingly told friends that if he couldn't find a real job, he would open a fruit stand in his hometown back in Douglas. And then it dawned on him that opening a hometown fruit stand was a mighty fine idea, considering Allegan County is a cornucopia of agriculture. Two weeks after graduating, Andrew opened Summertime Market, showcasing a bounty of produce from nearby farms.

"The purpose of the market is to make local food, grown all around us, more accessible, so I decided to take everything around that is good and local and bring it to one convenient location," says Andrew as a lunchtime customer grabs the last pesto chicken salad made by a topnotch caterer based in Holland, just up U.S. 31.

In July, the prime season here, people come for the freshly picked blueberries, sweet cherries, green and wax beans, German butter beans, new potatoes, beets, and truly inspiring heirloom tomatoes. A few of the market's participating area farms and their prod-

ucts: pasture-raised beef from Crestwick Farms in Ravenna; Grassfield's Cheese from Coopersville; Byron Meats from Byron Center; hearth-baked breads from Salt of the Earth in Fennville; gelatos and sorbets from Palazzalo's, also in Fennville; low-pasteurized, non-homogenized, certified-organic milk from Hilhof Dairy in Hersey; Koeze Cream-Nut peanut butter from Grand Rapids; and Sharon's Old-Fashioned Canned Goods from Harbor Springs.

There's a nice mix of customers here, too. You see Chicago vacationers bicycling there, delighted with their finds, locals looking for a fresh dinner ingredient, commuters swinging by for necessities, and couples putting together a beach picnic for the day.

Andrew sums it up: This has become the place to be. "It's amazing."

Coveyou Market, Petoskey

Coveyou Scenic Market might be the prettiest farm market in the state, sprawling out on the north arm of Ernest Hemingway's oft-mentioned Walloon Lake, with its 22 miles of visually arresting shoreline. Coveyou's 1940s barn perching on the bluff opens its doors onto a magical view.

"Makes you wonder who built the barn here; it has better view than the house," says David Coveyou. "I wish I had a way to research this, but National Geographic magazine in the 1960s did a Best Views in the Country piece, and they captured this farm. I have never been able to track it down."

The property was started as a homestead in 1874, and David, his wife, Kathy, with a little help from

"Makes you wonder who built the barn here; it has better view than the house."

from seed in late February to early March. In season, new potatoes are dug up every other day. The tomatoes—heirloom beauties—are plucked moments before the market opens for the day, he says.

In the barn, backdropped with Walloon Lake vistas, a wondrous tableau of homegrown produce is nestled in woven baskets on distressed and weathered wooden boxes. Nothing is wrapped in wasteful plastic here. You can almost taste how good it will be just by looking.

David says. "I get to church on Sunday—and fall asleep. We're plenty active."

David and Kathy vend at farmers markets in Boyne City, Harbor Springs, Charlevoix, and Petoskey. They also supply locally owned restaurants with herbs, vegetables, and flowers. In 2010 they launched their CSA, and it was a big hit, they report.

their three school-age sons, grow a stunning variety of pesticide-free produce, with magical sounding names such as eggplant varieties named Hansel, Gretel, and Fairytale, plus pattypan squash, eight-ball squash, and kohlrabi. "Everything is grown on the farm except the corn, (which) we bring in from another farm in Boyne City," David says. The herbs and vegetables are started

Each Tuesday "in season," 15 shareholders each pick up a CSA produce box with cool things to cook inside: Swiss chard, kohlrabi, fennel, and more. Kathy slips in a recipe or two.

David is hoping to awaken people from their standard dinner fare. "It's a great way to get more people using fresh vegetables, trying new things, and eating in season," says David, who farms about 20 acres of his 300-acre holding. "Every week, we're sneaking in something new that people have not had before."

Cheboygan Farmers Market

A pleasing handful of growers and taste-makers spread out their booths in the parking lot of the Cheboygan Opera House each Saturday morning in season. This is the Cheboygan Farmers Market. From June through October, they carry on a tradition of local trading that goes back centuries in these communities near the Straits of Mackinac. Buying and selling fresh produce here harkens back to another time when

transactions were face-to-face, local and personal, and you placed your money or trade good in the stained palm of a farmer you knew from down the road. Around here, the market also brings out the foodies who show up early, even before the tables all open, to pick out their summer-ripened corn, Japanese eggplants, muskmelons, peaches, raspberries, radishes, heirloom tomatoes, local eggs, small-batch honey, pure Grade A maple syrup, jams, and preserves.

A half-hour before opening time, grower Mandy Munger of Shifting Sands Farm faces a cluster of shoppers already hovering over her lovely stall. Her area is bright with the goodness of home-grown varieties she starts from seed in her hoophouse. Mandy's friend, Tina Clouser, stops by to buy sungold (orange-hued) cherry tomatoes, and the stall proprietor puts her to work.

With Mandy's toddler playing underfoot, the two women race about the three-table booth, packaging lush varieties like Sweet Ice corn, Ambrosial peaches, Walla Walla onions, Superstar muskmelons, purple-hued carrots, five colors of bell pepper, and lots of dried herbs for sale in pint Mason jars.

Every vendor has something indispensable that the addicted shopper simply can't live without. At the height of the season, the market brings out 27 farmers. Steve and Mary Crusoe of Golden River Orchards aren't there until the later weeks with the 11 apple varieties from their Cheboygan orchard. Sharone Jewell is an early arriver among the vendors, though. Alternately called the cake lady or the jam lady, Sharone sells assorted preserves and baked goods, including cakes, cookies, brownies, and quick breads.

Oryana Natural Foods Market, Traverse City

Established in 1973, the member-operated grocery (where guests can shop without joining) thrives through its sale of lovely items, from bins of fruits and vegetables to organic nuts and grains in bulk, snacks without fructose syrup, organic dairy products, and hormone-free meats. It's billed as the only food co-op in the country with its own soy-product brand, called Soyworks. Oryana's soy-based product, available in markets and restaurants statewide, starts with organic, Michigan-grown soybeans that are boiled and infused with sea minerals and fresh seasonings. This brightly lit, well-stocked wholefoods store offers organic everything, with helpful worker-members and the delicious Lake Street Café keeping the shopper engaged in the hunt for delicious products.

"We are proud to say we work with upwards of 80 local vendors, purchasing everything," says Sandi McArthur, Outreach and Education Coordinator. Guests will find food and beverage from Shetler's Dairy Farm in Kalkaska, Light of Day Organics loose leaf tea, Pleasanton Bakery, Land of Goshen cheese, and, apparently, about 76 more. On a visit to this "destination" store, my husband, Rich, adds to our cart a tasty looking growler (a small keg) of North Peak Brewing Co. root beer for our daughters, who are wan-

> ## "We are proud to say we work with upwards of 80 local vendors."

dering around the store and munching on summer-ripened peaches. Each visiting child gets to select a piece of fruit, which is a welcome improvement over the free-cookie policy some supermarkets follow.

Things certainly have changed since Oryana opened 35 years ago. Back then, it was started by a small group of families who were distributing sacks of brown rice and oats from a Traverse City back porch. From that, they became northern Michigan's only certified-organic retailer. Like a farmers market, Oryana offers member shoppers "food peace of mind" and an alternative to industrial-strength supermarkets.

Eastern Market, Detroit

Regulars to Eastern Market, the state's oldest continuous public market, wouldn't dream of missing this weekly shopping trip. It's a delightful crush of humanity — mothers pulling kids in red Radio Flyer wagons, fathers pushing strollers, fresh-faced joggers sporting the North Face label, food stamp (EBT) holders, couples with Blackberries, baby boomers with their adult children, and many immigrants who prefer the kind of farm-fresh produce reminiscent of their village markets. The Saturday market is always a big draw, bringing in as many as 40,000 people. Eastern Market is the centerpiece of a 40-block district that delivers an

growers, urban gardeners, small-food producers, and media teams prowling about with large microphones and video equipment.

The market has been here since 1891. In August 2006, the city management transferred the operational responsibilities to a public-private partnership called Eastern Market Corp. The enterprise is really three markets in one location: the weekly Saturday market, which most people are aware of; a special events venue for things such as Detroit Lions tailgating and the annual Michigan Beer Festival; and the wholesalers market, which runs from midnight to 6 a.m. Monday through Friday. The wholesale growers, some hauling their foodstuff in semis and others in pickups, sell to grocery stores and produce houses in the tri-state region.

The market sprawls across five sheds, each with its own theme. Built in 1896, Shed Two (Shed One was torn down), is the oldest but was nicely renovated in August 2008. Shed Three, built in 1922, was just refurbished for more than $6.5 million. Both sheds concentrate on food. Shed Four specializes in flowers, Five in other plants, and Six in landscaping. The renovated spaces

edible paradise to Detroit, sometimes called a "food desert" in certain neighborhoods because chain supermarkets operate exactly zero stores there. In those neighborhoods, people have to get what they can at the corner convenience store, which does not amount to much, or travel to the suburbs to buy staples.

The market's chaotic crowds are really something. Wholesalers and local farmers run 400 stalls hawking everything from a Peaches and Cream corn variety to purple fingerlings, Chinese long beans, Blazing Star peaches, green zebra tomatoes, farm-fresh eggs, whole organic chickens, handcrafted cheeses, and locally baked hearth breads. Eastern Market sprawls down six blocks in five sheds, all brimming with an astonishing variety of crops, plants, flowers, chef cooking demonstrations, curmudgeonly old farmers, cool organic

now are top-notch, with radiant-heat flooring, all-new restrooms, glass, and lighting. Randall Fogelman, vice president of business development for Eastern Market Corp., says the improvements were needed. "There is basically nothing we did not touch," he says.

"We define Eastern Market as the core encompassing fourteen acres, including the sheds and parking," Randall says. "But it is a 40-acre district made up of all the food businesses surrounding the marketplace, from meat processors, peanut roasters, distributors, produce houses to independently owned restaurants.

"People in Michigan have been eating local for a long time; we just didn't know it. Now everybody advertises it. They put Michigan-grown on their packaging," says Randall.

One corner of a main route through the market is an interesting and strong quartet of vendors: Avalon Bakery, Zingerman's Deli and Creamery, Vang Farm, and Grown in Detroit.

The Vang vending area, run by local Hmong Thai farmers, displays long beans, bitter melon, Thai holy basil, Thai eggplants, three varieties of bok choy (most Americans are familiar with only one kind—the one with the long green leaves and creamy-colored stem), and much more. Seller Yer Vang bundles bright blossoms into bouquets as her 15-year-old daughter, Kaew, and 17-year-old son, Chue, assist shoppers, many of whom are unfamiliar with the Thai produce but buying nonetheless. From Capac, about 30 minutes from Port Huron, Yer Vang and her husband and their seven children, farm the same vegetables her family grew in her homeland.

The Hmong people are members of the mountain tribes in Thailand who resettled in the United States after the Vietnam War. "When my parents moved to America, they knew they wanted to start a farm," says Kaew Vang, who is a sophomore at Capac High School. "Everything you see, we grow." For the Vangs, the Saturday market is a family affair starting with an early rising to load the truck, drive 90 minutes to Detroit, and spend all day in sales. At their booth, everything is carefully scrubbed, positioned and labeled—a visual draw for its beautifully exotic colors and textures.

At a nearby booth is the Holtz Farm. Since 1968, brothers Mel and Norm Holtz, who farm 60 acres in Ida, south of Detroit, truck to the Eastern Market and set up two sprawling stands to show off their fine produce, pastured-raised whole chickens, and farm brown eggs. The queue stretches away from their stalls because the Holtz brothers grow interesting varieties of produce, such as four sweet potatoes varieties, four beet varieties (including Bull's Blood, Golden, Red Ace, and white), a dozen heirloom veggie varieties, Cipollini onions, and pumpkins galore when in season.

Mel is asked about how he farms. "I don't know if the farm is sustainable. We'll probably go broke in the next few months," says the gruff guy with a comedic side. "I have been doing this my whole life. Farming is like being in the Mafia; it's hard to get out." Mel runs the family farm, which was established in 1870 by his ancestors from Germany. "They were originally headed for North Dakota. Glad they didn't make it. Michigan is cold enough."

As Detroit seeks to right-size itself with its shrinking population, some see urban farming as an opportunity to help map the future. For years, many Detroiters have grown tomatoes, greens, melons, and sweet dumpling squash in backyard plots, community gardens, and reclaimed vacant lots. Now, Greening of Detroit—a gardening collaborative—organizes market-bound produce from member urban farmers in a prime booth under the Grown in Detroit (GID) banner at Eastern Market. There, Grown in Detroit displays a staggering array of freshness, from collards, mustard greens, and eggplant to heirloom tomatoes in all their lumpy, pudgy, and flavorful glory.

> ## "It's about connecting around the things that are important."

Piggott's Market, Benton Harbor

In mid-September, about a month away from the season's first frost, a farm market on East Napier Avenue, a few miles from downtown Benton Harbor, is predominantly red, orange and green. Here's what's in season: summer's last tomatoes; jack-o-lantern types of pumpkins; assorted winter squash, including acorn, buttercup, Delicata, sweet mamas, and dumplings; and a dozen apple varieties from neighboring orchards. A sign provides each product's name and origin. The ever-bearing strawberries hail from Sodus, only a few miles away, peaches are from Coloma, and green beans are from Hartford.

"We grow about 40 percent of what we have here throughout the summer," says George McManus IV, who owns Piggott's Farm Market. "The other 60 percent comes from other farms located in about a 10-mile radius of our market. So everything is grown within Berrien, Cass, and Van Buren counties."

The recent Michigan State University graduate is called "Geo 4" by family to distinguish him from his dad, George McManus III (Geo 3) and his grandfather, George McManus Jr. (Geo 2). Geo 4 has been working at the farm market since he was a child. "We've been selling products by the road since the farm started in 1949," says Geo 4, who is 24 and has a bachelor's in agricultural business management with a minor in food-industry management.

Geo 4 says he understands the nuances of family farming, market retailing, and risk-taking. Geo 3 says he does, too: "It's a big risk to get started in agriculture. People don't realize that, because they will say it cost me next to nothing to put a garden in my yard. Well, wait until you do a couple of acres."

Geo 4 says he also knows he can take a little market share from supermarkets simply by extending friendship to the customers, many of whom really appreciate the effort the family puts into the market.

"Our customers are curious about everything. They come, they ask lots of questions, and they sincerely want to learn."

Ann Arbor Farmers Market

At twilight on a mid-September Saturday, the Ann Arbor HomeGrown Festival transforms the city's outdoor farmers market into a street party showcasing the best local growers, producers, taste-makers, and handcrafters. The stated goal is simple, and huge: spread the message that good food—drum roll, please—is a human right. This is a food community of farmers, growers, enthusiasts, home cooks, and chefs who structure their lives around the shared interest of food. Here are a few of the festival participants: a restaurateur who lists each locally sourced ingredient down to the exact farm; a CSA owner who slips recipes into members' weekly produce boxes; moms who only buy low-heat-pasteurized, non-homogenized milk and local eggs; and the home cook who roasts a heritage turkey for Thanksgiving.

"It's about connecting around the things that are important," says Kim Bayer, of Slow Food Huron Valley convivium (their name for a local chapter of the national Slow Food organization). "We have a chance to decide about the kind of future we want. I can't change the war in Iraq, the health-care system; but I can change how I decide to get my meat, how I decide to connect with my neighbors, or whether I choose to support a farmer. I can change the world, one bite at a time."

The event offers a marketplace with regional producers, restaurateurs, and others selling in a farmers market-style. It is a fine way to connect with and appreciate some of the Michigan people of the local-food movement. Here are a few of them:

—Eric Farrel of Ann Arbor, jam-maker extraordinaire of Farrell Fruit (supplies the popular Zingerman's Deli) who uses summer-ripened southeast Michigan fruits. Find him at www.farrelfruit.com.

—Simmons Family Farms, founded in North Branch in 1854, run by the fifth and sixth generations, scores big with its FarmBoy FlapJacks pancake mixes, cookie mixes, and organic tortilla mixes. Certified organic since 1996.

—Mill Pond, located on Sugarloaf Lake in Chelsea, makes kalamata olive twists with traditional

French sourdough, and Lithuanian rye bread made of organic stone-ground rye flour, 130-year-old rye culture, sea salt and water.

— Lunasa, an online local market connecting producers and hungry people through a website and twice-a-month pickup at its warehouse at 6235 Jackson Road, Ann Arbor. Shopping locally year-round from home; what a concept.

West Michigan Cooperative, Grand Rapids

On an icy January, the owners of Creswick Farms, Crane Dance Farm, Funny Farm Organics, and Little Red Rooster Bakery set up a loading dock with a plethora of hibernation foods, locally raised. For all those who believe food grown sustainably and closer to home tastes better, the West Michigan Cooperative is heaven-sent. Four years ago, four West Michigan Cooperative founders—Gerald Adams, Tom Cary, Paul DeLeeuw, and Gail Philbin—created the cyber market. They figured eating locally is something that can be done year-round. There are many ways now to extend the seasons, such as growing in greenhouses and hoophouses, or keeping produce in root cellars or atmosphere-controlled storage spaces.

Here's how the co-op works: For a full week, starting the first Sunday of the month, shoppers peruse the co-op's website listing the producers and their foods, including the usual variety plus fruit preserves, maple syrup, raw honey, freshly roasted coffee beans, soaps, woolen products, and dog treats. Everything is grown and produced in West Michigan using various farming practices from conventional to certified organic. Shoppers place orders online and pick up their items at the once-a-month marketplace, set up like a farmers market, with the producers bringing extra items for sale.

The online co-op's monthly pickup, affection-

ately called "Meet the Makers," becomes a warm, cozy party stocked with the region's best-known farm personalities. There's Kris Van Haitsma of Hudsonville's Mud Lake with her hydroponically grown salad lettuces, flat-leaf parsley, lemon thyme, watercress and microgreens that restaurants clamor for. Katie Brandt and Tom Cary of Groundswell CSA Farm of Zeeland heap their table full of fresh-from-the-farm winter produce, including red, Yukon Gold and Viking potatoes and butternut and Confection hybrid winter squash. Barbara Bull of Cherry Point Farm and Market of Shelby makes you wonder how you could possibly live without her cherry cabernet jelly, cherry almond jelly, and cherry-studded pastries.

Fulton Street Market, Grand Rapids

In the chill of early 2011, the Fulton Street Farmers Market in Grand Rapids tries something new: a winter farmers market once a month from January through April. On Jan. 7, which was a swirling snowy day, seven vendors smile as if spring were just around the corner and welcome shoppers to the outdoor market. Though blizzard-cold, shoppers turn out in respectable numbers, coming on foot, pulling red wagons, on bicycles with backpacks, and by car. The farmers and shoppers, surely the heartiest folks in the county that frosty Saturday, seem to feel the farmers market is the right place to be. Local food in the winter is something to celebrate, a reason to come down to the market. Extending the farmers market into the winter makes sense, considering farmers are prolonging their growing seasons these days with hoophouses and simple yet effective cold-weather storage. The new market also is fueled by an increased number of people who try to eat locally year-round with things that are appropriately seasonal. A few of the sellers:

—Case Visser, and his brother William, fifth-generation farmers of the well-known Visser Farm

started by great-great grandfather Marinus Staal in 1904 on Bauer Road in Jenison. The brothers stand in front of their trailer full of Chippewa potatoes, Red Delicious apples, brown eggs from William's Isa chickens, plus baskets of kale, rutabaga, turnips, and winter squash stored in a root cellar at their 120-acre farm in Holland. For Case, the Saturday winter market makes perfect sense. "Why go to a supermarket and buy produce when we've got local stuff year-round?" The Visser family sells at 20 farmers markets from West Michigan to northern Indiana. "Now we've got a way to get it to you (in winter)."

Pierre and Sharon Schierbeek of S&S Lamb out of McBain. Pierre and Sharon pasture-raise their lambs and goats without the use of chemicals, hormones, and antibiotics. "It's pretty much old-fashioned farming; it still exists," Sharon says.

At the biggest stall are Pat and Ginny Rakowski, of Wayand. They work out of a trailer filled with their grass-fed, pasture-raised meats, free-range eggs, pure maple syrup, dairy products from Mooville Creamery in Nashville (low-salt butter, milk, cream, ice cream), three varieties Michigan apples, root vegetables

"This is phenomenal."

(baby gold potatoes, carrots, rutabagas, Brussels sprouts). Shopper, Lucy Higuera, carrying three dozen empty egg cartons she wants to return to the Rakowskis, enters the farm trailer and laughs. "Are you charging admittance? It feels like a funhouse." Lucy is right about that, the hearty souls who battle the wintry weather for local-food-no-matter-what intend to keep small farmers in business. "I feel lucky to have this year-round," says Lucy who has eight children, meaning she and her husband go through a lot of eggs. "This is phenomenal."

Across from the Rakowski trailer, Bob Alt of Comstock Park displays four varieties of apples, including Fuji, Ida Red, MacIntosh, and Granny Smith. Finally, at River Valley Poultry Farm, Mark Schaub from Kingsley sells whole chickens and parts, various poultry eggs, and wild-caught whitefish from Mackinac Straits Fish Company.

Considering all these selections aren't shipped in or flown in from Peru or beyond, this is quite a selection of fresh foods for the middle of winter in Michigan.

From the Market Chapter Information

West Michigan Cooperative: 1111 Godfrey Ave. SW, Grand Rapids, MI 49503, (616) 951-3287, westmichigancoop.com and facebookcom/westmichigancooperative

Fulton Street Farmers Market: 1147 E. Fulton St., Grand Rapids, MI 49503, (616) 454-4118, fultonstreetmarket.org. Open January through April 10 a.m.-1 p.m. Saturday; and May through Christmas Eve, 8 a.m.-3 p.m. Tuesday, Wednesday, Friday and Saturday.

Summertime Market: Blue Star Highway at the Bridge, Douglas, MI, (269) 857-8568,summertimemarket.com and summertimemarketblogspot.com. Open daily 9 a.m. to 7 p.m. May until around November.

Coveyou Scenic Farm: 4160 US 131, S. Petoskey, MI 49770, (231) 348-1278, coveyouscenicfarm.com

Cheboygan Farmers Market: City Hall parking lot, Cheboygan, MI, 49721, (231) 627-8815. Open June through late October or early November, depending on the harvest.

Oryana Natural Foods Market: Community cooperative since 1973, 260 East Tenth Street, Traverse City, MI 49684, (231) 947-0191, oryana.coop. Open 7:30 a.m.-8 p.m. Monday through Saturday and 10 a.m.-6 p.m. Sunday.

Detroit Eastern Market: 2934 Russell Street, Detroit, MI 48207, Public Market Hours: 5 a.m. - 5 p.m., Saturday, and 11 a.m. - 7 p.m. Tuesday in Shed Two (corner of Russell and Winder Streets) from July through September. (313) 833-9300, www.detroiteasternmarket.com

Piggott's Farm Market: 3824 E. Napier Ave., Benton Harbor, MI, tomatofresh.com. Open 9 a.m.-6 p.m. daily May through October.

Ann Arbor Farmers Market: Located in the historic Kerrytown District, 315 Detroit St., Ann Arbor, MI 48104, (734) 794-6255, a2gov.org/market. Open January through April 8 a.m.-3 p.m. Saturday; and May through December 7 a.m.-3 p.m. Wednesday and Saturday.

FROM THE KITCHEN

Beyond the obvious pleasures of a great plate of dinner, I've always been vitally interested in food and its place in our lives. I take such delight in these things: pouring my own batch of fragrant fruit puree into hot canning jars, picking way too many blueberries because I just can't stop, growing butternut squash to add warmth and color to our fall dinner table, and rescuing those last tomatoes on the vine before the first killing frost.

When dining out, I'm endlessly curious about everything and agonize over the menu choices. I wonder about the chef's preparations and procedures, I try to pinpoint ingredients while tasting a dish, and I yearn for a bite from other peoples' plates.

When traveling, I keep a journal about every restaurant, farmers market, bakery, and random treat that comes my way. I often paste menus right into the journal, and I could tell you down to the garnish what I've enjoyed where and when. Such pleasures they are, too: the fresh-fruit smoothies and soppas in Puerto la Cruz, Venezuela; seafood in Venice during a carnival there; a hearty bushtucker (any native-food dish) in Australia; up-market gastro pubs in the English countryside.

I like to say that I come by this food passion honestly, because my father, James Beeler, started his "restaurant life" at age 15, working in establishments from our hometown of Louisville, Kentucky, all the way to Scottsdale, Arizona, where he now works at the Scottsdale Hilton Villas and Resort. Also, my grandmother Odessa Moore retired from a lifetime of cooking at Spalding University in Louisville. As you might imagine, it is a parade of Southern deliciousness at our family reunions, Thanksgivings, and Kentucky Derby Day gatherings.

Now, more than ever, culinary adventuring is a major part of the travel business. In Michigan, agri-tourism is ramping up for more visitors than ever to all-local-food restaurants, markets, and more. Food tourists want to view the livestock where it is raised, they want to eat farm-to-table dinners outdoors, take cooking classes, and learn all about the land. Yes, corn mazes and you-pick operations have been running for years, but today's agri-tourism takes a more educational form. People learn about working farms, they get out in the pasture where the goats are grazing, watch as the goats are milked, and follow the product through to the cheese phases in the kitchen. These are the places where people are falling in love with good, local food that's coming From the Kitchen.

Eateries and local suppliers

Selling cuisine from the community—raised by local gardeners and farmers—is a year-round challenge that takes dedication to do well, and visitors love hearing the story these days of how a farm or a restaurant is making a go of it.

One longtime Traverse City business is a good example of how local food comes to the kitchens. To help their guests understand the culinary wonderland of northern Michigan, Grand Traverse Resort and Spa partnered with a firm called Learn Great Foods, led by Ann Dougherty, to conduct tours of the Old Mission Peninsula, Leelanau Peninsula, and the region. With its rich soil, moderate microclimates, and pristine waters, Grand Traverse County produces fine produce, meats, cheese, and wine that have great stories to tell during culinary tours. The area's farmers, vintners, and tastemakers throw open the barn doors to day-trippers and vacationers on the tours.

"We've been doing 'local food' around here (since) before it had a name," says J. Michael DeAgostino, public relations manager at Grand Traverse Resort. Whatever it takes to find the right ingredients is what resort staff has done for years, he says. "We've been driving to farm stands where you help yourself to seasonal fruits and vegetables and put your money in the coffee can sitting out."

"Traverse City has been known for cherries for a long, long time. Then the wineries came into prominence," he says. "All of a sudden, it wasn't just cherries, and wine regions inspire a more sophisticated cuisine because chefs and farmers discover a common interest. Werp Farms is a great example. They started growing the specialty crops the chefs were asking for (and it started) a great synergy between restaurants and agriculture."

Elsewhere, to help city and suburban food touring, Ann Wilson's Culinary Escapes, based in Royal Oak, operates walking tours in the Detroit area. A recent Royal Oak tour took in nearly a dozen spots, including the lively local farmers market, the third-generation Superior Seafood market, the farmstead restaurant Café Muse, Gayle's Chocolates, Hermann's Bakery and more.

"We're getting people enthused about Michigan and its culinary destinations," Ann says. "This is about walking and sampling the extraordinary in our communities, at locally owned restaurants, farmers markets, bakeries. We're moving beyond conversation and showing people that Michigan is both a top agricultural state and culinary stop."

Michigan kitchens are making so many wonderful taste treats, and I will start with a few of my favorites right here: farm-to-table restaurants popping up all over, golden-good raw honey, artisan gelatos, small-batch jams made from scratch, crusty breads fresh from the oven, and top-tier chocolates for a touch of luxury. Let's look a little closer at some of these favorite things from the kitchen.

Zingerman's Edible Landscape

When it comes to making seriously crusty artisan breads, with fragrant aromas and firm honeycomb texture, Zingerman's Bakehouse ups the ante on the flavor factor. Their operation is mind-boggling in its size. Every day the young bakers make about 4,000 loaves and during holidays, as many as 12,000. That's more than a million loaves a year. Stopping by Zingerman's Deli is but one way to buy incredible bread. Take it from me, go for the brilliant trifecta of the Rustic French Farm

Creamery, making assorted cheeses and gelatos, relocated from Manchester and Zingerman's Coffee Company moved to Plaza Drive. In the back of the Bakehouse, Charlie Frank began handcrafting chocolate candy bars called Zzang bars, launching Zingerman's candy manufactory. A year later, BAKE! the hands-on teaching bakery (bakewithzing.com), and CAKE!, cake showroom, squeezed between the bakehouse and creamery. Zingerman's, the little Deli that could out delicious all the others, included Zingerman's Mail Order business; management-training company, ZingTrain; and Zingerman's Roadhouse. This farmstead restaurant is run by Alex Young, a prestigious James Beard Foundation Best Chef-Great Lakes Region nominee, who started a garden behind his house to supply the restaurant.

bread, leavened with Frank's sourdough, with its thin crispy crust and soft chewy interior; Parmesan Pepper bread loaded with a quarter pound of aged Parmigiano Reggiano and cracked Telicherry black peppercorns; and Pecan Raisin stuffed with a half-pound of pecans and raisins that makes a mighty fine piece of toast. If you live in Michigan, venture out to Zingerman's Bakehouse near the Ann Arbor Airport.

"We did not have a vision for retail here," says Katie Frank, bakeshop manager. "It's not zoned for retail, but people kept turning up because they knew we were baking bread here for the Deli. They would come and want to buy bread, so we though we should try to service them." At Zingerman's, one good thing always leads to another. The bakery, opening in 1992 with Frank Carollo at the helm, is one of the eight companies that make up this $35 million powerhouse. Zingerman's

"We never compromise on quality," says cheese and gelato maker, Josh Miner, as he sets up the elaborate cheese display. "Stay as long as you like, but I have to pull the lemon gelato out." Yum! I guess it's impolite to offer to lick the spoon.

So, on that drizzly August morning, we moved into Zingerman's Bakehouse. Fresh-baked aromas waft around the production of whole-wheat farm, three-pound loaves with crisscrossed domes, thin crispy French baguettes, luxurious braided challah and chocolate cherry bread sweetened with Belgian chocolate and

Michigan dried cherries. Every loaf goes into the French Fringand baking oven which contains 40,000 pounds of brick and mortar in the bottom to maintain even heat. The loaves are baked on stone to create a nice crust. With 12 doors, the impressive workhorse bakes 360 loaves at a time. It's all superlatives—impressive, hearty, and sumptuous. They pay attention to everything.

Like a stage performance, each worker is choreographed to capture the exuberant rise in every loaf, knowing the bread makes the moves. One shapes baby sized, 1-½ pound loaves, another sprinkles bread flour into the German-made willow bread rising baskets which imprints deliciousness into every loaf, others hand-score flavorful character into the Sicilian Sesame Semolina loaves. With the music cranked to deafening levels, they waltz about measuring pound upon pound of flour, salt, and those wonderful enhancements such as Michigan dried cherries, unhulled sesame seeds, Vermont cheddar, New Mexican green chilies, Parmigiano Reggiano and southern pecans that bedazzle

the breads. In the pastry workroom, Gary folds fresh red raspberries into pastry cream. Jeremy shapes macaroons and Devonie sprays 24 large and 96 small Bundt pans for the Summer Fling (coconut lime) coffeecakes.

Zingerman's Deli, which brought extra-virgin olive oil, dark roast coffees, and European cheeses to the forefront, helped show us the taste possibilities. They have this whole deliciousness thing down-pat. For a long time, they have been roasting single-estate, small batch coffee beans, handcrafting cheeses with cow's milk from Calder Dairy in Lincoln Park and Green Meadow Dairy in Elsie, and offering tons of olive oil from Italy, Spain, Greece, and France to California, Chile, New Zealand, Australia and South Africa.

An edible landscape surrounds Zingerman's Deli, a gorgeous 1902 brick building, where lush greens and herbs bloom into ornamental prettiness and kitchen practicality. In the well-tended garden the basil, lavender, sage, rosemary, thyme and marjoram deliver spectacular scents and handsome leafy stalks. The Zingerman's experience certainly involves all the senses, making everything deliciously three- dimensional. "Our mantra is full-flavored and traditionally made," says Rick Strutz, managing partner who joins Ari Weizweig and Paul Saginaw. Zingerman's Deli opened on March 15, 1982, when they began making their sandwiches and cutting cheeses in a teeny-tiny space with five tables and four stools. Then, Ari and Paul visioned out a business plan called "Zingerman's 2009: A Food Odyssey" to foster its identity and business growth without sacrificing its uniqueness. Now they're working toward 2020, considering Asian street food, traditional Tunisian fare and a microbrewery. "Were always thing of quality," Rick says.

Filled-with-wonder breads

Avalon International Bread's mantra of "Eat Well, Do Good" is a fitting philosophy for owners Ann Perrault and Jackie Victor, who caused quite a sensation in Detroit when they turned a dusty old brick building into delicious destination of sweet yeasty aromas, rustic European loaf breads, and taste treasures such as their sweet cream scones. There's a vegan peanut butter cookie, too, studded with Callebaut chocolate chips. Ann and Jackie gave their creations names that were connected to the history of the city they call home. Dequindre Cut trail mix cookies are named after an abandoned railroad line transformed into a multi-use path. The cookie is a breakfast of sorts; a classic oatmeal cookie, but

studded with dried cranberries, raisins, sunflower and pumpkin seeds. Farnsworth Family Farm sourdough, Corktown cinnamon raisin, and Leelanau cherry walnut are named for the area, too. In June of 1997, with a lot of hope and $6,000 borrowed from friends and family, Ann and Jackie opened their doors in the Cass Corridor of Detroit, launching more than artisan breads, it turned out. They helped inspire a neighborhood revival of caring and homey comfort, one storefront at a time. Embraced by Detroiters seeking locally grown businesses and foods, Avalon sparked a turnaround and attracted a good chunk of hungry people from the suburbs to West Willis Street (visit shop-midtown.com). Now, from dawn till dusk, more than one-thousand customers stream through the doors seven days a week. Every morning, three trucks deliver to 40-plus restaurants and markets stretching from Ann Arbor to Grosse Pointe. Calling Avalon a "right livelihood business" means Jackie and Ann care about the triple bottom line; the "Three E's" of (social) equality, environment, and (local) economy.

Stone House Breads: In 1995, former Detroit newsman Robert Pisor started this bakery to hand-form the perfect loaf of sourdough bread with four ingredients: organic flour, well water, sea salt, and Leelanau County sourdough. "We do make bread the old-fashioned way, with

dough is turned onto long tables where seven to eight bakers knead and form loaves by hand. On delivery day, they mold 4,000 loaves of various shapes and textures, including breads called Asiago cheese, Traverse City cherry walnut, rustic Italian, and garlic fougasse. Try Stone House's granola, sweetened with Traverse City cherries and Leelanau County honey, delivering gustatory crunch. "We have been voted the No. 1 statewide bakery in Michigan, by the Detroit Metro Times, and we're not even in the Detroit market. But we're aiming for it," says Tonie, who delivers bread to nearly 100 grocery and retail outlets in the state.

Pleasanton Brick Oven Bakery in Traverse City, in the former state hospital firebarn known as Building 66, bread-makers Gerard Grabowski and Jan Shireman craft their golden wheat bread made from just five ingredients: organic unbleached white, whole wheat and whole rye flour, plus water and unrefined salt. They make a gorgeous loaf, light in color and texture and with a terrific hint of rye. If you find some whole-wheat bread too dense and heavy, this is the loaf for you. Pleasanton, with the region's only wood-fired brick oven, creates naturally leavened breads, a full line of organic sweets, and a variety of savory baked goods. The bakery space is part of the Hearth of the Village at Grand Traverse Commons—an impressive and beautiful urban renewal and historical renovation project.

sourdough," says new owner Tonie Zahn-Spearing. "Our 'mother' (sourdough) was born at Leelanau County, surrounded by the Manitou Islands, cherry orchards, and sunlight. It's our belief when the mother was born, she absorbed the fresh healing air of Leelanau County and has been alive for these many years." That's not the only thing they do differently here. The bakehouse's only equipment is a large mixer to combine the purest ingredients. Not a single preservative can be found here. The

Wealthy Street Bakery: In 2002, next-door neighbors David and Melissa LaGrand and Jim and Barb McClurg scrubbed up an old liquor store in a forgotten part of Grand Rapids. They installed a spectacular brick oven and set about baking crusty, flavorful breads that were an instant sensation. Customers love the hearth-baked breads, pizzas, pastries, scones, and puffy cinnamon rolls thick with icing.

"From the start, our goal has been to create the kind of bread we love to eat. Bread with real flavor and personality; bread we couldn't find anywhere in the area," Melissa says. "We thought it would take a while for people to find us and believe in us, but they lined up as soon as we opened the doors. Grand Rapids was dying for great bread. The biggest thrill has been creating a place where people come and go all day long. We love how much life our bakery has added to Wealthy Street."

They had to start opening earlier in the mornings because commuters wanted to drop by on the way to work. Soon, the bakers mentioned to some neighbors that a storefront next door was for sale, and so Amy and Steve Ruis opened the Art of the Table kitchen, fine foods, and wine shop. Now, the whole stretch of Wealthy Street features home and living stores, a farmstead restaurant, a coffee roaster, a yoga studio, upmarket salons, a sustainable foods grocer called Nourish and an independently owned bookstore. Man cannot live on bread alone? That's right. But bread can sure start some good things happening.

Hermann's Bakery: This is the kind of old-school bakery where the second-generation owner, Richard Hermann, makes American sandwich bread. You know, the fresh, white bread with a thin crust baked in a metal pan. His cinnamon bread swirls with sticky good stuff, just like you'd expect. Richard fills his Royal Oak store with unsliced sandwich breads, rustic-style yeast breads, pastries, cookies, and 20 kinds of coffeecake. Standing next to a cooling rack that's emptying fast, Richard cleverly draws us in with a story about his dad.

"See, Dad was laid off, sitting in the pool hall, keeping warm," Richard explains. "Things were different back then. Someone came in and said the baker needs a helper, and Dad, who was 19, was the first one here. He started out washing dishes, became a partner in 1929, and bought it outright in 1942." Young Richard grew up at the bakery, playfully kneading pie dough and first learning how to make little tarts.

His seasonal coffeecakes, made with Michigan fruits of the season, from strawberries to apples and award-winning holiday scones, are snapped up quickly, but Richard remembers the days when he couldn't make bread fast enough, either. In those days mothers sent their children and husbands off in the morning with a belly full of toast and a brown bag with one or two sandwiches. Nowadays kids get lunches at school and people don't make sandwiches at home nearly as much anymore, he says. So Richard concentrates on the coffeecakes, seasonal fruit kringle, doughnuts, and seasonal cookies.

Eateries that grow kitchen gardens

Winchester At Wealthy: The cooking here is ingredient-driven and starts in the restaurant's vegetable garden. Looking for inspiration, executive chef Nick Natale starts his workday in the garden, because what's ripening there helps shape what appears on the menu. Everything is influenced by the bounty of the garden—pizzas topped with cherry tomatoes, local goat cheese, roasted peppers, and basil. Or try the kitchen-made pierogies with Swiss chard, tomatoes, and onions from the garden and andouille sausage from Sobe Meats. Or the Winchester basil pesto slathered on flatbread made at Winchester.

"Right now, the beans are ready, so I try to work them into as many dishes as possible," says Nick, plucking beans and popping them into a sack. "The beginning of my shift is when I put together the specials."

The garden, formerly a paved-over Grand Rapids city lot between two rambling Victorian houses, consists of 12 raised beds full of enriched soil. For Winchester at Wealthy owners, Paul and Jessica Lee, growing some

of the restaurant's food was the next logical step. The energy it brings to the chefs, the restaurant, and the neighborhood is exhilarating. Jessica grows a mouth-watering selection of items, such as a dozen varieties of heirloom tomatoes and five kinds of peppers, including habanero chile, kung pao chile, albatross, red and green bell peppers. A row of leafy green herbs, basil, and flat-leaf parsley stretches upward. A cluster of tomatillos, green beans, eggplants, Brussels sprouts, and pumpkins stretch along tidy, weed-free rows. Jessica, who grew up on a Cheboygan farm, finds peace and purpose in the garden. "When I want to take a little break, I come out here and pull weeds," she says. "I love maintaining this little space."

Paul likes it, too, that the garden has been a "core value" of the restaurant business. "We wanted to be involved in every aspect of this garden. This really forces us to think outside the box, because we're dealing with produce that is fresh today. It's never been refrigerated or bundled in little rubber bands."

The garden started a relationship with the neighbors, who liked the idea of the vacant city lot transformed into a green garden. Paul and Jessica brought in heavy equipment, pulled out the concrete, piled on top-quality soil, and built the raised beds.

"We want the restaurant to be a neighborhood place for the people who live nearby. We want people to walk in and say, 'Hey, this is my place.' Our philosophy is all about making that connection," says Paul, who has big ideas about the future of Winchester at Wealthy.

Woodbridge Pub: At the start of summer, Woodbridge Pub restaurateur James "Jim" Geary looks around his property for a sunny spot to grow heirloom tomatoes. His search leads him to the building rooftop. "It's full-sun all day long," says James, who wants better tomatoes than the mass-marketed, industrially farmed ones offered through the food service. He is after a riot of colors and full-sensory flavor. And bring on the lumps and bumps, the fuzzy, funny, striped and mottled tomatoes of yesteryear; many of those early varieties were incredibly good.

Up a simple ladder he built, James hauls a total of 40 (10-gallon) containers and enough organic soil to fill them. He mixes in fine and rough composts, vermiculite, and a topping of mulch. "I've learned a lot this first year," he says. "Next year, we will do a better job with structural support so the plants don't fall over. I've learned a lot about pruning, when to harvest, how long fruit keeps." Now, in the height of summer, every day brings a harvest of wet, wild, luscious, tomatoes in different sizes and shapes: Green Zebra, oxheart-shaped Anna Russian, Cherokee Purple, Eva's Purple Ball, Red Zebra and Brandywine, to name just a few.

"We try to make it spectacular."

"This is the smell of summer," he says, holding up a harvested prize. "A minute ago, it was on the vine. You don't find tomatoes like this at the store or in restaurant kitchens." Woodbridge Pub's caprese salad is crowded with multicolored, summer-ripened tomatoes, from-scratch mozzarella, and fragrant basil from a community garden across the street. In September 2008, through lots of sweat equity, James renovated an abandoned Detroit party store into a warm, fascinating restaurant. In a sense, James reclaimed the space, renovating and salvaging everything from the bar (back door from an old house in Saline) to the wainscoting, (from the choir loft of an 1890s Saginaw church) to a walk-in cooler (from a butcher shop in Hamtramck), now the men's room, and bits from an Art Deco bowling alley helped create a unique floor. "It's a really good vibe," James says of the interior.

James, who grew up on his family's farm in Salem, dreams of farming five acres in the city and opening a farm school to teach old-fashioned agriculture. "I would love to teach city kids about food, where it comes from, how it's raised; to understand that macaroni and cheese made with powdered cheese isn't real food. It's funny, because we now know it's all about educating. When we introduce a new seasonal menu, some of the customers wonder what happened to this or that," he says. James finds local sources when possible for the menu items, including breads from Avalon Breads International, salad greens and herbs from Brother Nature Produce, and greens and berries from Gass Farm in Romeo.

From farmstead to eatery

Trattoria Stella: This neighborhood restaurant and bar in The Village at Grand Traverse Commons has quite the northern Michigan pedigree. The daily "fresh and local" menu lists the farms providing the sourced ingredients, including these: the Friske Orchard for Cameo apples and rhubarb; Land of Goshen for eggs, goat cheese, ground pork, and pork shoulder; Shetler Dairy milk, and Majszak Farm for maple syrup. The burrata pugliese menu selection is a standout. Chef Myles Anton, a 2010 James Beard Award semifinalist for Best Chef/ Great Lakes, wraps freshly made ricotta in a pillow of house made mozzarella cheese, nestled in tomato brodo, shaved Prosciutto di Parma, and summer-ripened tomatoes. The sophisticated/rustic combination promotes the farmstead cuisine the chef believes in. Myles delivers American farmhouse cooking at its most creative, exciting best. Take the gnocchetti for example: slow-cooked pork shoulder twirled with caramelized onions, fried sage, and wilted spinach; a dish that makes the most of those surrounding farms. This white-napkin, farm-to-table restaurant housed in Traverse City's sprawling old state hospital uses interesting spaces, with the brick-lined hallway becoming some of the best seats in the house. The restaurant's vast wine list also features some

Michigan creations, and craft beers are on tap, too. This is the kind of place you can order anything on the menu and be happy with the result.

Salt of the Earth: At this rustic American eatery and bakery, Chef Matt Pietsch isn't fooling around with the safe and familiar. He is a nonconformist and proud of it. Here in Fennville, a little Allegan County village a bit inland from Lake Michigan, Matt applies classic techniques to southwest Michigan's bounty of fresh of ingredients. Salt of the Earth is surrounded by small family farms committed to growing great produce, plus excellent farmers markets selling heritage meats, farm-fresh eggs, farmstead cheeses, and more. This is a hip, intimate space with exposed brick walls, warm woods, heavenly wood-fired aromas, and one talented chef. Matt is a true believer in the gospel of locally grown ingredients who charges through Michigan's four seasons, butchering Berkshire pigs, filleting wild-caught Great Lakes fish, and serving summer berries, stone fruit, and heirloom vegetables of every stripe.

Salt of the Earth's core menu, which changes four times a year, focuses on the fresh and exciting. There's often a seasonal spin to wood-fired pizzas, farmer greens, soups, wild-caught fish, heritage meats and poultry, and the wonderful Southwest Michigan Milkshake featuring Palazzolo's Artisan Gelato & Sorbetto gelatos whirled with fresh fixings. A fresh board also shows daily specials shaped by what's ready right now. "Sometimes we don't want to put something that has a two-week window or season into our core menu," Matt says. "We might not be able to rely on it. But the fresh board allows us to change it up and work creatively. Last week, on the fresh board, we supported 23 farmers, growers and producers, and that doesn't include Michigan wines, beers, and spirits at the bar." The July 9 menu, for example, included items from local growers and producers Evergreen Lanes Creamery, Boeve Farm, Creswick Farm, Mud Lake Farm, Eco-Acres, Kismet Organics, Palazzolo's Artisian Gelato and Sorbetto, Boetsma, Russ Latchaw, Blackhawk, **and** Cisela farms. That's a whole lot of relationship-building.

Matt, along with owners Mark Schrock and Steve Darpel, established solid relationships with many farmers, producers, and taste-makers. They built on the farm-to-table relationships that Journeyman Café, the

"We like to celebrate that bounty of local food around here, so everything is house made. Everything is hand-prepped. Here, we don't buy bags of chopped up anything. We grind our own burger, make our sausage, cure meats, bake our hearth-baked breads, make catsup, make mayonnaise, hand-roll pasta, and smoke a lot of things. Everything we do isn't 100 percent local, but we try to make it spectacular."

previous restaurant in the space, had developed. "I don't want to say we didn't have to work at it, because we do, but a lot of these people find us. Two or three farmers a week get in touch with us. Every once in a while, we'll get a knock on the door, and there's somebody with a truck full of stellar produce (saying) 'Hey, look at what I've got,'" says Matt, who also shops at the Holland and Saugatuck farmers markets for the fresh board.

Around here, it's all for one. The community rallied around Mark and Steve as they worked to establish their restaurant in the space formerly occupied by Journeyman Café, which closed a few years ago. "There was the sense that something was missing, that we needed a farm-to-table restaurant here; that something good had to happen," Mark says. So now they are challenging the status quo; how we think of food, and what and where we purchase. "It's not new; rather it's the old way of doing things," Matt says.

Café Muse: In Royal Oak, the slow-braised rabbit with housemade chorizo and exotic mushrooms comes from Suchman Farms in Tipton. The vanilla pancakes stuffed with blueberry mascarpone come from Carbon's Golden Malted in Buchanan. When in season, the smoked Gouda scramble with tomatoes and basil comes from Royal Oak Community Farm. The mixed greens with goat cheese, curried pecans, and buttermilk cider vinaigrette come from Werp Farms in Traverse City. The old-fashioned milk products hail from Crooked Creek Dairy in Romeo. Quite a list of food origins, in fact, and restaurateurs David Smith and Greg Reyner visit each purveyor, walking the land and asking about the product. They are building a community around food, opening people's eyes to the links between, say, Royal Oak Community Farm, a nonprofit maintained by volunteers, and Sun Ra Farms in Traverse City, and the food on their plates. They don't get all preachy about it, they just let the menu do the talking.

Greg, the executive chef and a Master Gardener candidate, creates innovative comfort foods with the freshest, purest ingredients he can find. Together, Greg and David built an agri-infrastructure to support their local-foods menu. "It's not only important for our economy but for us, as owners, to inspire our guests with Michigan's amazing ingredients," David says. "The cost of bringing fruits and vegetables from California, Mexico, or even Chile is crazy. Special high-quality foods, that we prefer, just don't travel well."
Café Muse is a pleasant space with 60 seats, nearly 40 more than its previous location down the street, incorporating Italian Renaissance paintings, plush velvets, and a high purpose for the menu. This do-good restaurant that promotes edible change, seems to be working very well. They actually have groupies. "I have never worked or done something in my life where I get so many hugs," David says. "People come up to us and hug us all the time. They love the food. They love the space. They love the farm-to-table connection."

On a recent Tasting and Touring visit to Café Muse, we love the food, too, including Greg's peanut butter, jam, and mascarpone cheese sandwich dressed with honey and vanilla. "The secret is the honey; Michigan honey produced by a 16-year-old, home-schooled kid whose parents challenged her to come up with a business for an assignment," David says. Mallory's Busy Beehive, out of Silverwood, produces raw, unfiltered honey that Café Muse can't get enough of. Moving on, we sample Oprah's favorite thing—grilled three-cheese sandwich dripping with fontina, havarti, and mozzarella cheeses, basil, honey, and summer's finest tomatoes between organic bread from Detroit's Avalon International Breads. Café Muse's profile went sky-high after Oprah Winfrey and *Esquire Magazine* raved about the delights to be savored there.

How sweet they are

Palazzolo's Artisan Gelato And Sorbetto: Fennville's Palazzolo Gelato beats Willy Wonka and his factory stuff any old day. On our tasting visit, we feel like the real Golden Ticket winners as we tour the facility. Time and again, we stop in our tracks to take in the fascinating gelato and sorbet production. You can't help but be impressed by the mounds of glistening berries and stone fruits, chocolate, premium tree nuts, and rich liqueurs. In big mixing bowls, heaps of red raspberries and white chocolate swirl into fluffy clouds of vanilla gelato. In the bakehouse, apple pies from the nearby Crane's Orchard and bakery are chopped into large chunks to fold into a novelty pie gelato. On the main production floor, one worker grinds hazelnuts into a paste for a spiced treat with ginger, nutmeg, and fig pieces; another whirls tree-ripened peaches into a frozen piece of heaven; another buries Mackinac Island fudge into an ice-cold bowl of pana gelato. We taste and we taste; thank goodness no Oompa Loompas pop up to kick us out.

"This is the real deal. We can't fake these flavors," says Pete Palazzolo, our Tasting and Touring guide for the day. "If you think about it," he says, "if you are going to make raspberry gelato and you're not a chemist or at some company with a laboratory, it would be pretty difficult to fake it. To make the raspberry sorbet taste like raspberries, we put in so many that it can't help but taste (right)."

Palazzolo's churns out 600 flavors, all-natural, without additives, working in small batches using fresh dairy products from local cows. Palazzolo's goes to great lengths to make things right for its product line, which is known and sold far and wide. "When we put cookies in our gelatos, we first make the cookie. So I put in a bakery so we can do just that," says Pete. Most of the wonderful flavors concocted here are based on delicious, locally grown fruits and/or his Italian heritage, he says. One scoop at a time, Pete has become one of the top gelato-makers in the nation. As a high-schooler in 1986, while working at his mother's Italian-cuisine restaurant in Saugatuck, Pete amazed customers with his hand-crafted Italian gelatos (softer and denser than American gelatos) and sorbettos (made without eggs or dairy). The silky, fresh-flavored gelatos were a hit from the start, Pete recalls. As the frozen treats quickly became a focus of the business, his mother closed the restaurant and Pete opened his whole-sale business, expanding from a few ice-cream parlors and restaurants to serving thousands of accounts nation-wide and abroad. Now, Palazzolo's has product labels in many languages, including Arabic ones for sales in

Egypt, he says. "They found us and felt our products would work because their consumers like quality at an affordable price point." Pete says.

Pete is running two businesses in one these days. The food production side churns out the tasty stuff for restaurants, scoop shops, bakeries, and grocery stores; the restaurant-supply side sells equipment, display cases, booths, and professional consulting for shop owners about lay-out and design.

From a simple notion of making a great product from local sources, has grown a company of more than 50 employees, he says. This is an example of a Michigan agricultural business helping to fuel the local economy and provide meaningful jobs making a great product. "My heart is in this every step of the way," Pete says. "I know I'm the luckiest guy in the world."

Green Toe Gardens Honey: Some of Rich Wieske's best honey comes from colonies right next to Eight Mile Road, at Detroit city limits, in hive yards along Rosa Parks Boulevard. Plenty of flower stock in the area is fueling the bees, Rich says. Plants growing in Detroit's patches of urban greenery include exciting nectars of aster, daisy fleabane, goldenrod, sedum, and black locust. Honey bees are so attracted to the fragrant nectar of nearby linden trees that they are called "bee trees," Rich says. "This is really something that is good. Bees are absolutely the most important part of the food chain."

Rich produces raw and unfiltered honey he likes to call "Virgin honey, because it's not pasteurized. Go to a grocery store, and the honey is all liquid and will stay that way for months because it's pasteurized, which destroys the natural crystals." Raw, unfiltered honey also retains pollen, and some allergy sufferers believe eating honey close to home helps them develop immunities, or at least a measure of resistance, to nearby pollen types.

"I'm a bee activist. My goal is to get as many urban beekeepers going as possible," says Rich, who runs a bee school with detailed, six-class sessions as well as one-time workshops for schools, scouts, garden clubs, and community groups. "Detroit is 140 square miles, and a third of that is vacant land which makes great forage for honey bees. There are a lot of natural places in Detroit; a very, very productive place for honey bees."

Rich took up beekeeping to harvest honey for his mead-making. Mead, the oldest fermented beverage, was mentioned by Plato, before the time of Christ. It is made of honey, water, and yeast, with alcohol content similar to wine.

"Once I got up to 120 gallons of mead a year, I decided I needed a cheaper source of honey," says Rich, of Royal Oak. "So we started with two hives…which became four, then eight." Most beekeepers will add a couple of new hives each year to increase production, but Rich doubled his numbers until he reached 100. "Fortunately, bees are very self-maintaining. They lived

for about 60 million years without us, and they (still) do pretty well without us."

Rich's Green Toe Gardens gathers product from hives placed far and wide, from inner city Detroit to the Straits of Mackinac. Why so many locations? The flavor and aroma of a local hive's honey is derived from the flowers on which the bees feed in that area, Rich says, so hive placement is a high art. He bottles the prized star-thistle honey from Kalkaska and "Troll Honey" from Bliss, about 20 miles south of the Mackinac Bridge. Troll Honey is flavored with basswood, star thistle, and goldenrod. Other great tastes include an alfalfa honey and red clover honey, both from St. Charles, and blue-berry blossom honey from Berrien County.

Rich, who is a local mentor through the Southeastern Michigan Beekeepers Association, con-siders honey a kind of medicine. Ingesting pollen and honey is better than getting a flu shot, he claims. "Pollen is probably the single highest source of protein in na-ture. It's almost 30 to 33 percent protein. It contains 95 percent of the amino acids, minerals, enzymes, and vitamins a person needs. Honey and pollen together is almost a complete food. Humans could live on that. In fact, St. John the Baptist lived 40 days and 40 nights on milk and honey. We don't think about it. Check the diet of any Olympian who gold-medals. They are quaffing honey drinks and pollen because you get energy; a rise -- not a spike. And because honey is a complex sugar, your system doesn't have to process it. It's right there and ready for use when you need it."

Looking ahead, Rich seeks to try queen-rearing, to breed queens better-suited for Michigan. He explains that only about a third of the queens shipped from California, Georgia, and Texas survive a full year in our harsher climate. "We're trying to get in a situation where we can raise our queens and stock on local sources. It's really another way to make it homegrown and local."

Jam Lady: In the Keweenaw Peninsula, the loveliest, wildest berries—thimbleberry, blueberry, huckleberry, raspberry, and chokeberry—grow in crazy places, in the kind of knotted overgrowth where you have to combat-crawl your way in to pick a few. "When you find three or four, you think you've hit gold," says Paul Mihelcich, of the Jam Lady in Eagle River, near the shores of Lake Superior. Yes, the "Jam Lady" is really a man, a dude, a guy. Paul is a former Army man, too, so don't make any wisecracks…but if you compliment him on his wonderful jams, all cooked and packed by hand, he'll share with you a very nice story 75 years in the mak-ing. Paul is proud to be the second male to operate this small-batch, specialty jam business. After his mother, Florence, passed away, his dad, John, happily took on Florence's title of Jam Lady.

Paul cooks jams and thinks of the business the way his mother and grandmother, Genevieve Butkovich, did. "My grandmother used to have this wooden farm-stand out on the road, about a mile and half from where we are now," Paul says. "At that time, the thimbleberry jam was a nickel, and wild strawberry was a dime. She would go out there, put out jars and a little can. Then, later on, she'd go back and collect the money." Back in the 1970s, when Paul's mother took over, the state decid-ed that jams for sale must be produced in a licensed kitchen, so Florence complied and soon needed to come up with a busi-ness name. Because ev-eryone called

pectin. "There are no real secrets, although we did have to develop some of them by trial and error," Father Basil says. "Making jam in small batches with only sugar—no high fructose corn syrup—helps ensure good flavor, as does the intensity of the wild fruit."

It's all fatiguingly purist here. In summer, everyone rises at 5 a.m., celebrates Divine Liturgy beginning at 6, and starts work in the kitchen by 8. The doors of the Jampot store open at 10, and the sales room and kitchen operate until 5 p.m. Thirty minutes after that comes Vespers, then dinner, more work for the store, and then sleep. The next day, more of the same.

The days weren't so busy when Father Basil and Father Nicholas from Detroit settled at Jacob's Falls in the Keweenaw Peninsula. They moved in shortly before Labor Day.

"The first order of business was surviving our first winter—which we almost didn't," Father Basil says. "Beyond that, we had no clear idea of what we would do the following spring. We knew a monastery had to support itself through the work of its monks and that the work had to be done at the monastery itself; working at jobs outside

the monastery would be self-defeating. Thinking about it during that long cold winter, we could come up with nothing better than picking wild berries and selling jam, as did many people in the area at the time."

It was the summer of 1984 when Father Basil and Father Nicholas started making jam in an old restaurant building near Jacob's Falls. The monks scrubbed up the kitchen, a few kettles, and some tongs and got down to business. They spent the days gathering thimbleberries,

raspberries, blueberries, chokecherries, and pincherries; evenings found them in the kitchen, prepping, cooking, and cooling batches of the fruit. "Because serious picking is a full-time job and there were only two of us, we were unable to have a retail outlet, so we sold everything we produced to a distributor. The 120 or so cases, maybe 1,500 jars, we produced that first year barely covered expenses for the summer months. But it was a start."

The next summer was cold and rainy, with a poor harvest, but they managed to produce slightly more than in their inaugural season. Their distributor ran into money troubles, though, and couldn't buy the product. After scrambling to find other outlets, the two resolved to market the jam themselves. In 1986, they opened Jampot and got some help with the picking so one of them could man the shop in the afternoons. By 1987, the store and kitchen became their full-time work, so they bought from local pickers and began to make a few baked goods, too. Today the popular bakery makes up about half the business, all of which supports the monastery.

"Keeping up with everything has been quite a challenge," Father Basil says. "We struggle to keep up with the demand."

Mindo Chocolate Makers: Jose Meza and his wife, Barbara Wilson, run one of the few bean-to-bar chocolate factories in the country. They start with shade-grown cacao beans from Jose's native Ecuador. They are partial to the cacao-tree varieties called nacional or criollo, considered to bear the finest quality beans. The Nacional only grows in Ecuador. In a bit of a kismet, the two practically stumbled into these flavorful Ecuadorian bean varieties. The couple were celebrating their 30th wedding anniversary with a six-week trip through Ecuador and checked out the Amazon basin where the cacao trees originated. "We fell in love with the little town of Mindo, located in the Andes Cloud Forest," Barbara says. Before long, in 2007, they bought a little piece of land in Mindo, which is known as one of the best bird-watching places in the world. Somehow the little house they dreamed of turned into a hotel and restaurant called El Quetzal de Mindo.

"Making jam in small batches..."

Barbara started experimenting with chocolate-making at that point, from the cacao beans right out of the pod to the finished chocolate. She really wanted to make brownies in the restaurant. After playing around with different percentages, she turned up a winning formula. Soon, she added her chocolate to the restaurant's menu. Interestingly enough, cacao trees don't grow in Mindo because the elevation is too high, so they found themselves in Puerto Quito. Jose and Barbara hooked up with an Ecuadorian farmer who grows certified organic cacao trees interspersed through a rain forest. "He is probably the best farmer down there. He harvests the cacao beans and gives them to us fresh," says Barbara, who holds dual citizenship here and in Ecuador. "Right out of the pod, which is the delicious stuff." It was important for Jose and Barbara to find an eco-conscious farmer who cared about environmental stewardship.

They take only the best cacao pods back to their small farm in Mindo, where the beans ferment for six days in fermentation boxes and dry for one to three weeks, depending on the weather. They control the fermentation process that is critical for developing the smoothest, best-flavored chocolate, making sure the beans are not exposed to any contaminants. The beans then are roasted, ground to nibs, and winnowed at their Mindo facility or one they operate in Michigan, in Dexter. The cocoa nibs, or dried cocoa beans, are shipped to the Dexter chocolate kitchen, where they are transformed into chocolate, cocoa butter, and cocoa powder. "Very few people in the country do this," Barbara says.

In Dexter, Barbara makes 77-percent chocolate bars with chocolate liqueur, organic evaporated cane

juice, and cocoa butter. That's it. She also skips shelf-life-extending additives. Barbara also is known for her dark chocolate brownies, bars studded with dried fruit, and cocoa powder.

"We fell in love with the little town of Mindo..."

Patricia's Chocolate: At Patty Christopher's chocolate laboratory, you can feast your eyes on trays of artisan ganache and caramel chocolates studded with dried Grand Traverse cherries, Black Star Farms cherry brandy, Grand Haven strawberries, dried Michigan blueberries, and so much more.

In a midcentury-modern house in Grand Haven, Patty turns out some of the best chocolates around. In her licensed commercial kitchen, Patty, a retired public school psychologist, works with almost frightening devotion, creating delightful chocolates favored by very discerning clients. To name a few: Before bedtime, Black Star Farms bed and breakfast places a mini-box of Patricia's Chocolates on each guest pillow. The Cook's House in Traverse City serves a duet for dessert. Art of the Table in Grand Rapids and Grand River Grocery in Ada snap them up fast for their loyal customers. Patty routinely makes thousands of her artistic chocolate gems by hand and gives "chocolate talks" far and wide.

No two of Patty's chocolates are alike, even those of the same type, because each is hand-made. "I am the only one that touches every aspect. They are hand-crafted from beginning to finish," she says.

Patty is always introducing new beauties to her line, currently at 28 varieties, including lemon cardamom, salted butter caramel, maple star anise, apple cinnamon caramel, and ultra dark cognac, "which also has a Michigan raw honey. It's a 91-percent dark ganache. It's really amazing," she says. Patty's new Michigan chocolate bar is shaped like the Lower Peninsula, with the major rivers outlined. She also pipes a little red heart onto the particular city where she's selling the chocolate bars and customizes the label with green and white for Michigan State University and maize and blue for U of M. Both are sold at the main campus museum shops. The mitten-shaped bar is embedded with Michigan dried cherries, Michigan dried blueberries, pistachios, and fleur de sel. Also new are espresso tiles made with beans from Great Northern Roasting Company in Traverse City. The tile shards are excellent for eating out of hand or garnishing a lovely dessert.

Patty trained at Chicago's prestigious French Pastry School with the French chocolatier Pierre Herme and U.S. artisan producer Norman Love. She takes classes at the Callebaut Chocolate institutes in Chicago and Montreal. With the help of her husband, Paul, she turned the lower level of their Grand Haven home into a chocolate studio, full of fine European chocolate instruments. A shelf displays the liqueurs she uses, including Black Star Farms cherry, apple, and pear brandies, aged Cruzen rum, Cassis liqueur, tawny port, and aged tequila. Pure Michigan maple syrup and raw honey join the grouping.

The chocolate kitchen by creating an "enrobing room" with an "I Love Lucy" machine that enrobes the chocolates and caramels. This machine from France includes a little conveyer-belt system just like in the classic Lucy skit. During a recent visit to view the contraption at work, Patty takes a tray of Earl Grey Tea chocolate squares infused with bergamot orange oil and dark and milk chocolate and places the treats one at a time on the Savy-Goisseau machine. As the squares march through, they are enrobed with pure dark chocolate. She places a transfer sheet of colored cocoa butter that works like a stick-on tattoo to imprint each gorgeous candy. Afterward, each ganache and caramel chocolate resembles a mosaic of design, indicating the flavor to be found inside.

The chocolate kitchen features a U.S. made ultra-high-speed food processor, a ganache-cutting unit from Germany, and much more in the way of gadgets. Patty is over the moon with excitement about her latest endeavor. She says she is one of seven people in the world with access to making chocolate from a long-thought-extinct cacao bean, called Fortunato No. 4. "Cacao beans are only grown 15 to 20 degrees on either side of the Equator, so they only grow in a certain part of the world, and the United States isn't one of them. They're grown real close to the trunk of the tree; and when you break them open, the mushy pulp is what you're after. That is fermented and dried out on racks, then covered with banana leaves at night to keep away moisture and dew. Eventually, all of this white, mushy stuff drains off, and you're left with little prized beans that become luscious chocolate."

To get such visual, sensual, and elegant results, Patty pays attention to everything. After she developed wrist pain from repetitive hand-dipping, she expanded

"People say all the time that the chocolate looks too pretty to eat. This is sort of my gift. I have never thought of myself as being artistic, but I am really attentive to detail." Her individual chocolates are 30 by 30 millimeters, which is larger than the standard 22.5-

millimeters treats, so she searched a lot to find the right boxes. Her origami-like boxes from Asia add to the artistic element. She has diligently trained each retail store employee to carefully arrange the chocolates in the box before they are covered with layers of glassine paper and thick candy pad to protect the contents. Many retailers add the flourish of a fancy bow to finish the wonderful presentation.

Patty suggests slicing each precious square into quarters, which are a great way to savor the taste and identify the flavors. "I recommend when cutting to get a clean swipe each time," Patty says while demonstrating.

"This is fresh mint leaf infused in dark chocolate and heavy cream, then enrobed in rich dark chocolate. The fresh mint is grown in pots right outside that window."

A lovely story that Patty likes to tell helps sum up the emotional factor of this line of work: "I had a girl, a teenager, try my chocolate. Like so many people, she just closed her eyes (while tasting). She opened her eyes, smiled, and said 'That just makes me happy.' Well, being a retired psychologist who worked in the public schools and private practice, I know that an indulgence can make you happy, can create a positive emotion."

From the Kitchen Chapter Information

Zingerman's Delicatessen: 422 Detroit St., Ann Arbor, MI 48104; (734) 663-3354; zingermansdeli.com. Open everyday 7 a.m.-10 p.m.

Zingerman's Bakehouse: 3711 Plaza Dr., Ann Arbor, MI 48108; (734) 761-2095; zingermansbakehouse.com

Avalon International Breads: 422 W. Willis St., Detroit, MI 48201; (313) 832-0008; avalonbreads.net

Stone House Breads: 2425 Switch Drive, Suite B, Traverse City, MI 49684; (231) 933-8864; stonehousebreads.com

Pleasanton Brick Oven Bakery: 811 Cottage View Drive, Traverse City MI 49684; (231) 941-1964; pleasantonbakery.com

Wealthy Street Bakery: 610 Wealthy St. SE, Grand Rapids, MI 49503; (616) 301-2950; wealthystreetbakery.com

Hermann's Bakery: 317 S. Main Royal Oak, MI 48067; (248) 541-3218.

Grand Traverse Resort and Spa: 100 Grand Traverse Resort Village Boulevard, Acme, MI 49610; (231) 534-6000; grandtraverseresort.com

Winchester At Wealthy: 648 Wealthy St. SE, Grand Rapids, MI 49503; (616) 451-4969, winchestergr.com

Woodbridge Pub: 5169 Trumbull St., Detroit, MI 48208; (313) 833-2701, woodbridgepub.com

Trattoria Stella: 1200 W. 11th St., Traverse City, MI 49684; (231) 929-8989, and stellatc.com/stellatc

Salt Of The Earth: 114 E. Main St., Fennville, MI 49408; (269) 561-SALT   saltoftheearthfennville.com

Café Muse: 418 S. Washington Ave., Royal Oak, MI 48067; (248) 544-4749; cafemuseroyaloak.com

Palazzolo's Artisan Gelato and Sorbetto: 413 Third St., Fennville, MI 49408; (269) 561-2000 and (800) 4GELATO; 4gelato.com.

Green Toe Gardens Honey: Product available on the first and third Saturdays at Royal Oak Farmers Market, 316 E. 11 Mile Road, Royal Oak, MI (248) 246-3276; and Avalon Breads International

Jam Lady: 50555 State Highway M26, Mohawk, MI 49950; (906) 337-4164, thimbleberryjamlady.com

Jampot: 6500 State Highway M26, Eagle Harbor, MI 49950, societystjohn.com

Mindo Chocolate Makers: Sold at retail locations in Ann Arbor, Chelsea, Dexter, Detroit, Grass Lake, Holland and Kalamazoo; online store at info@mindochocolate.com. Dexter, MI 48130; (734) 660-5635; mindochocolate.com

Patricia's Chocolate: Sold at retail locations in Kent and Ottawa counties. Grand Haven, MI 49417; (616) 842-5999; E-mail: patricia@patriciaschocolate.com

Recipes

Asparagus-Parmesan Tart   188

Strawberry Caramel Pots 189

Buckwheat-Honey pancakes   190

Triple berry sandies 191

Latitudes Cranberry Bean Hummus 192

Black-eyed peas with collard greens and tomato broth   193

Glazed Pork Chops 194

Roast Chicken 194

Cranberry meringue pie 195

Von Norasing's cherries and cream tart 196

Roasted Pear Sauce 197

Kismet Farms Pear Custard Cake 198

Christmas Cove apple pie 199

Whitefish chowder 200

Cider-roasted lamb leg 201

Big Jim's Meatballs with Spaghetti 202

Roast Vegtable Frittata 203

Zingerman's Roadhouse Macaroni and Three Peppercorn Goat Cheese 204

Goat Cheese Mousse in Parmesan crisps 205

Julee Rosso's Raspberry Blueberry Bread Pudding and Vanilla Sauce 206

Summertime marinara sauce 208

Jaye and Terri's Garden Pesto 208

Oven Roasted Tomatoes 209

Rob Burdick's Roasted Winter Squash Halves 210

Eggplant Caponata 210

Stone House three cheese-tomato sandwiches 211

Café Muse in Royal Oak Braised Short Ribs 211

Ricotta gnocchi with tomatoes and rosemary 212

Royal Oak Spinach Salad 213

Asparagus-Parmesan Tart

All-purpose unbleached flour, for work surface
Half of a 17.3-ounce package Pepperidge Farms Puff
Pastry Sheets (1 sheet), thawed according to package
directions
1½ pounds fresh asparagus, trimmed
Extra-virgin olive oil for drizzling
Sea salt and fresh ground pepper
1 cup fresh grated Parmesan cheese

PREPARATION: Heat oven to 400 degrees. Line a baking
sheet with parchment paper. On a floured work surface,
roll out puff pastry to a 15-by-10-inch rectangle. Trim
uneven edges, but keep excess dough handy. Place pastry on prepared baking sheet. With a sharp knife, score a 1-inch border around pastry and form double-thick sides with the excess dough. Pierce dough all over with fork. Bake until dough starts to color, about 7 to 9 minutes. Remove from oven and reduce heat to 350.

Trim the asparagus to fit the tart. Arrange asparagus on the puff pastry, alternating spear ends. Drizzle with olive oil and sprinkle with sea salt, ground pepper and Parmesan cheese. Bake until puffed and golden, about 20 minutes. Cool slightly.

Makes 8 appetizer servings.

Strawberry Caramel Pots

CARAMEL SAUCE

1 cup granulated sugar

Up to ¼ cup of water

6 tablespoons unsalted butter

½ cup heavy whipping cream

FILLING

Unsalted butter for buttering

2 to 2½ pounds strawberries, halved (if large, quartered)

Half of a 17.3-ounce package Pepperidge Farm Puff Pastry Sheets (1 sheet), thawed according to package directions.

Whipped cream for serving.

PREPARATION: Heat oven to 400 degrees. To make the caramel sauce, in a heavy-bottomed 2-quart saucepan over medium high heat, combine sugar and water until the sugar has dissolved. Bring to a boil. Immediately whisk in butter until dissolved and continue to bubble along until the mixture darkens to an amber color. Remove from heat and slowly whisk in heavy whipping cream.

Lightly butter 8 ramekins in either ¾ or 1-cup measure. Evenly distribute strawberries in the ramekins and add 1 tablespoon caramel. (Save remaining caramel sauce for another use, i.e. ice cream). On a lightly floured surface, roll out puff pastry just enough to even out the folded lines. Cut 3½ inch rounds from the pastry and place on top of the strawberries. Place the dishes on a rimmed baking tray and bake the tarts for 20 minutes or until the pastry is puffed and golden. Enjoy straight from the ramekins or turn the tarts out onto plates and top with whipped cream to serve.

Makes 8 servings

Buckwheat-Honey Pancakes

1 ¼ cups buckwheat flour

¾ cup unbleached all-purpose flour

¼ cup granulated sugar

1 teaspoon cinnamon

2½ teaspoons baking powder

½ teaspoon baking soda

¼ teaspoon salt

1 tablespoon honey

2 (possibly 3) eggs

1 cup buttermilk

3 tablespoons unsalted butter, melted

Pure maple syrup to serve

PREPARATION: In a large mixing bowl, sift together flours, sugar, cinnamon, baking powder, baking soda, and salt. Make a well in center. In a separate mixing bowl, beat together honey, eggs, buttermilk, and melted butter. Gradually add wet ingredients to the dry mixture, beating between additions.

Ladle pancake mix onto hot griddle ¼ cup at a time. When bubbles open and stay open, it is time to turn over pancakes. When no steam escapes from edges, they are done. Serve with pat of butter and pure maple syrup.

Makes 4 to 6 servings.

TRIPLE BERRY SANDIES

1⅓ cups unbleached all-purpose flour

⅔ cup whole-wheat pastry flour

⅓ cup packed light brown flour

¼ teaspoon baking powder

¼ teaspoon salt

½ pound (2 sticks) unsalted butter, chilled and cut into small pieces

¼ cup dried cherries, coarsely chopped

¼ cup dried cranberries, coarsely chopped

¼ cup dried blueberries

PREPARATION: Heat oven to 350 degrees. In a mixing bowl, combine all-purpose and whole-wheat flours, brown sugar, baking powder, and salt. With a pastry blender, cut in butter until mixture resembles coarse crumbs. Stir in cherries, cranberries, and blueberries. Turn dough onto clean, dry work surface and gently knead (about 5 good kneads) until dough holds together without crumbling. Divide dough in half and, using parchment paper, roll each half into a log about 2 inches thick. Wrap each in plastic wrap and freeze.

Later, unwrap dough, let stand at room temperature for 10 minutes. With a sharp knife, slice each log into ¼-inch slices. Place 2 inches apart on parchment paper-lined baking sheet. Bake 16 minutes or until edges are firm. Transfer to a wire rack to cool completely.

Makes about 3½ dozen cookies.

LATITUDES CRANBERRY BEAN HUMMUS

2 cups cranberry beans simmered in vegetable stock until
beyond al dente
1 tablespoon tahini
¼ cup vegetable stock
¼ cup sautéed onion
1 teaspoon cumin
1 tablespoon extra-virgin olive oil
Salt and pepper to taste
Orange zest and blood orange-infused olive oil for
garnishing

PREPARATION: Strain beans of cooking liquid. In the bowl of a food processor, combine beans, tahini, vegetable stock, sautéed onion, cumin, and olive oil. Pulse until smooth. Season with salt and pepper. Using a rubber spatula, transfer to a decorative serving bowl. To serve, make an indentation in the center of the hummus with a large spoon. Sprinkle on the orange zest and drizzle the blood orange-infused olive oil.

Makes about 2 cups.

From Latitudes Roadhouse & Steelheads Tavern, Howard City, Michigan

Black-eyed peas with Collard Greens
and Tomato Broth

1 cup black-eyed peas

1 tablespoon olive oil

2 onions, chopped

2 cloves garlic, peeled and chopped

1 medium-hot or 2-3 mild fresh chiles, chopped

1 teaspoon ground cumin

1 teaspoon ground turmeric

9 ounces fresh or canned tomatoes, diced

2½ cups chicken, beef or vegetable stock

½ cup chopped cilantro leaves, divided

½ pound collard greens, boiled in salted water, 20

minutes until tender, drained and chopped

Juice of ½ lemon

Pita bread, to dip

¼ cup crumbled feta cheese

PREPARTION: Put the beans in a pan, cover with cold water, bring to a boil and cook for 5 minutes. Remove from the heat, cover, and leave to stand for 2 hours. Drain the beans, return to the pan, cover with fresh cold water, then simmer for 35 to 40 minutes, or until the beans are tender. Drain and set aside.

Heat the oil in a pan, add the onions, garlic, and chile; sauté for 8 minutes, or until the onions are just browning. Stir in the cumin and turmeric first, then the tomatoes, stock, half the cilantro, the beans, and chopped collard greens, then simmer for 20 to 30 minutes. Taste for salt, then stir in the lemon juice and remaining cilantro. For serving, sprinkle the top with feta cheese and serve with the pita bread.

Makes 4 servings.

From Anja Mast of Trillium Haven CSA in Jenison, Michigan

GLAZED PORK CHOPS

4 center cut pork chops, each about 6 ounces
and ¾ inch thick

2 tablespoons oil, preferably soy

Sea salt and freshly ground pepper

10 fresh sage leaves, thinly sliced, divided

½ cup apricot or peach jam or marmalade, divided

PREPARATION: In a large skillet, heat oil over
medium-high. Season pork chops with sea salt and
pepper to taste and add the pork chops to the skillet.
Cook until browned, about 2 minutes per side. Reduce
heat to medium, add half of the sage and jam/preserves
onto the chops. Turn and add remaining sage and jam/
preserves to the other side. Cook until desired doneness,
for about 2 minutes.

Makes 4 servings.

ROAST CHICKEN

1 (3½ to 4-pound) chicken

1 apple, quartered and cored

1 onion, peeled and quartered

1 clove garlic, peeled and smashed

Handful of leafy green herb, oregano, rosemary,
tarragon, parsley, sage

4 tablespoons unsalted butter, melted

Sea salt and freshly ground pepper

1 cup chicken stock, white wine, apple cider or water

ROAST CHICKEN PREPARATION: Heat oven to 400
degrees. Rinse chicken, then dry it very well with paper
towels, inside and out. The less it steams and the drier
the heat, the better. Stuff the cavity with the apple, onion,
garlic, and fresh herbs. Rub the chicken with butter, about
4 tablespoons.

When salting the bird, "rain" the salt over the
bird so it has a uniform coating for a crisp, salty skin
about 2 tablespoons). Season with pepper and place in
the pan with either 1 cup chicken stock, white wine,
apple cider, or water. Rotate the roasting pan every 15
minutes. Roast until a meat thermometer inserted in the
breast registers 160° and the thickest part of the thighs
reads 165°. As soon as the chicken is cool enough to
handle, without removing it from the pan, slice the meat
into the pan juices.

Makes 4 servings.

CRANBERRY MERINGUE PIE

FILLING

12 ounces (about 3¼ cups) fresh cranberries, or frozen, thawed

1¼ cup granulated sugar

¾ cup orange juice

Pinch of salt

One-eighth teaspoon ground cinnamon

⅓ cup quick-cooking tapioca

MERINGUE

4 large egg whites

½ teaspoon cream of tartar

¼ cup granulated sugar

PREPARATION: In a large saucepan, bring cranberries, sugar, orange juice and ¾ water to boil. Reduce heat and simmer for 5 minutes, stirring occasionally, until cranberries pop (about 5 minutes). Pour through a mesh strainer, pushing liquid through and discarding the rest. Return the drained mixture to the saucepan. Stir in salt and cinnamon. Whisk tapicoa into cranberry mixture; bring to a boil over medium heat, stirring constantly. Reduce heat and simmer 10 minutes. Pour into pre-baked pie crust. Heat over to 350 degrees. With an electric mixer on high speed, beat egg whites and cream of tartar until soft peaks form, about 5 minutes. Slowly add sugar and continue beating until stiff peaks form. Spoon the meringue over the pudding and make Curly-Q's with a spoon throughout thc mcringue. Bake for about 5 to 10 minutes or until meringue lightly browns. Watch closely— do not let it darken. Transfer to a wire rack to cool completely. Cover, refrigerate and chill at least four hours..

PREBAKED PIE CRUST

1½ cups sifted, unbleached all-purpose flour

½ teaspoon salt

½ cup shortening

4 to 5 tablespoons ice cold water

PREPARTION: Heat oven to 400°. In a medium bowl, mix flour and salt. With a pastry blender, cut in shortening until mixture looks like coarse meal. Add cold water (fluff with fork) until dough no longer clings to sides of bowl. Roll out on a lightly floured surface to a 12-inch round. Transfer dough to a 9-inch pie plate. Trim to about ½-inch beyond edge of pie plate; fold under and crimp edges decoratively. Prick bottom and sides all over. Bake for 10 to 12 minutes. Makes 8 servings.

VON NORASING'S CHERRIES AND CREAM TART

CRUST

2½ cups unbleached, all-purpose flour

½ teaspoon salt

1 tablespoon granulated sugar

½ pound (2 sticks) unsalted butter, chilled and cut into small pieces

2 tablespoons vegetable shortening

Up to ½ cup ice water

FILLING

2 to 3 cups tart (sour) cherries, fresh or frozen fresh, pitted if desired

1 cup granulated sugar

5 egg yolks

¼ cup sour cream

½ cup heavy whipping cream

½ cup unbleached, all-purpose flour

1 teaspoon vanilla extract

PREPARATION: To make the filling, with a food processor, pulse the flour, salt, and sugar. Add butter, a few pieces at a time, pulsing after each addition. Add shortening, then ice water, a little at a time, until the dough can be formed into a ball. Flatten out the dough into a round disc, wrap in plastic and refrigerate for about an hour. Position a rack in the middle of the oven and heat to 350 degrees. Roll out the dough in between two plastic sheets. Butter the bottom of an 11- or 12-inch tart pan with removable bottom. Press the dough evenly over the bottom and up the sides of the pan. Prick a few holes in the dough with a fork, then line the dough with parchment paper and fill with pie weights or dried beans. Bake about 15 minutes. Remove from oven and cool.

   Line the tart crust with cherries. Cover the entire bottom with a few more cherries on top of the first layer. In a medium bowl, combine sugar, egg yolks, sour cream, cream, flour, and vanilla. Whisk until well-blended. Pour the mixture over the cherries and bake for about 45 minutes or until slightly brown on top.

Makes 10 to 12 servings

ROASTED PEAR SAUCE

4 pounds pears, peeled, cored, and cut into eighths

2 tablespoons unsalted butter, melted

½ teaspoon ground cinnamon

¼ teaspoon ground nutmeg

2 tablespoons pure maple syrup

PREPARATION: Place the oven rack in the middle position and heat oven to 350 degrees.

Place pear pieces in shallow baking pan. Toss with melted butter, cinnamon, and nutmeg. Cover tightly with aluminum foil and roast 35 to 40 minutes.

Uncover once or twice to stir. Uncover the pan and roast for the final 5 to 10 minutes, until the fruit feels quite tender when tested with a small, sharp knife. The pears will be puffed slightly, steaming profusely, and exuding juices. Drizzle with maple syrup and stir briefly.

For chunky sauce, smash the pears with a potato masher. For smooth sauce, place the pear mixture in the food processor and pulse once or twice.

Makes about 4 cups.

From Mari Reijmerink of Kismet Certified Organic Fruit Farm in Fennfille, Michigan

Kismet Farms Pear Custard Cake

8 tablespoons (1 stick) unsalted butter, plus more for buttering pan(s)

1½ cups all-purpose flour

¼ teaspoon kosher salt

1 tablespoon baking powder

¾ cup granulated sugar, divided

¾ cup milk

3 eggs, separated and at room temperature

1 teaspoon vanilla

2 cups ripe (but firm to the touch) Bartlett pears, about 2 large or 3 medium

Parchment paper

Muffin tins (2 dozen) or 2 (6-inch) cake pans

¼ cup granulated sugar mixed with 1 teaspoon vanilla extract (add more sugar if necessary to have a moist sand consistency)

PREPARATION: Heat oven to 350 degrees. For muffins, lightly butter or line two standard (12-cup) muffin pans with paper or foil liners. For petite cakes, lightly butter two (6-inch) cake pans, and spray bottom with nonstick cooking spray and line bottom with parchment paper. Set aside.

In a medium bowl, whisk together flour, salt, baking powder, and half of the sugar. Set aside. Melt butter until fully melted and hot. Set aside. In a large bowl, whisk together milk, egg yolks, and vanilla. By hand, beat the wet mixture until frothy, about 3 minutes, and pour in the still-warm butter, whisking constantly about 1 minute. The finished mixture will appear separated and clotted, Whisk longer if it has not separated. Set aside.

Next, peel the pears leaving the nicest skin (50% maximum), remove core and slice pears into ½-inch pieces. In a large bowl, combine the pears with the flour mixture, tossing thoroughly so all pears are well-covered in flour mixture. Set aside. Using an electric mixer, whip egg whites until frothy, then slowly add the remaining sugar. Beat to soft peak stage, glossy and soft, yet able to hold a point. Add the wet mixture, stirring first, to the pear flour mixture, folding until just combined (five or six strokes). Take half of the whipped egg whites and fold into batter (four to five strokes), until it is evenly loosened. Fold in remaining egg whites using as few strokes as possible (five to six). Batter will not look smooth. Divide into prepared pans and sprinkle the vanilla sugar evenly over the top.

Bake until toothpick comes out clean (no batter). Take care not to test in a pear piece. For muffins, bake 25 minutes. For cakes, bake 35 minutes. Cool muffins for 5 minutes and cakes for 10 minutes; remove cakes from pans. Makes 24 muffins or two (6-inch) cakes.

From Mari Reijmerink of Kismet Certified Organic Farm in Fennville, Michigan

CHRISTMAS COVE APPLE PIE

CRUST

2½ cups sifted, unbleached, all-purpose flour

1 teaspoon salt

⅔ cup plus 3 tablespoons well-chilled Crisco All-Vegetable Shortening Baking Sticks

5 to 6 tablespoons ice cold water

FILLING

6 to 8 cups apples, preferably Pippen, Gravenstein, Wealthy, or Wolf River

1 cup packed light brown sugar

5 tablespoons unbleached, all-purpose flour

½ teaspoon cinnamon

⅛ teaspoon nutmeg

2 tablespoons butter, sliced

PREPARATION: To make crust, combine flour and salt in a mixing bowl. With pastry blender, blend cubed, chilled shortening into flour until it resembles coarse crumbs. Sprinkle ice cold water into flour; gently mix with a fork. Add more flour if necessary until dough holds together. Gather dough into two balls (one larger than the other). Flatten balls into disks. Wrap them in plastic and chill for 30 minutes. Position a rack in the bottom of the oven and heat to 400 degrees. Meanwhile, to make filling, peel, core, and cut apples into ¼-inch-thick slices. Placed peeled apple in a large bowl. Stir in brown sugar, flour, cinnamon, and nutmeg.

Roll out the larger dough ball on a lightly floured surface to a 12-inch round. Transfer the dough to a 9-inch pie plate. Spoon the filling into crust. Dot with butter. Roll the second ball out on a lightly floured surface to a 12-inch round. Drape the crust over the filling. Press the overhanging top and bottom crust together, then fold the edge under to be even with the edge of the pie dish. Crimp the edges decoratively. Cut slits in the top crust.

Bake on a rimmed baking sheet until the crust is golden and the filling bubbling thickly in the center, about 1 hour.

From Phyllis Kilcherman of Christmas Cove Orchards in Northport, Michigan

MICHIGAN WHITEFISH CHOWDER

4 cups water
3 bay leaves
1-½ pounds boneless whitefish fillets, cut into chunks
3 strips bacon
1 large yellow onion, diced
½ cup celery, diced
½ - 1 teaspoon dried dill weed
¼ teaspoon fresh ground black pepper, or to taste
Salt to taste
2 to 3 cups whole milk
3 medium-size Michigan Chippewa potatoes, peeled and diced
½ pound smoked whitefish sausage, sliced
2 cups fish stock or clam stock
1 tablespoon minced chives for garnish

PREPARATION: In a large, heavy-bottomed skillet, combine water, bay leaves and fish fillets. Bring to a boil, reduced heat and simmer about 10 minutes, until fish is cooked through and liquid is steaming. Transfer fish to a shallow bowl and cover to keep warm. Reserve 2 cups of cooking liquid and bay leaves. Fry bacon in a Dutch oven until crisp. Transfer to a paper-toweled lined plate. In the Dutch oven, remove all but 1 teaspoon of bacon fat and sauté onion and celery until onion is translucent. Do not brown the onion and celery mixture. Add reserved cooking liquid, bay leaves, dill weed, pepper and salt to taste. Bring to a boil, then reduce heat and simmer about 10 minutes to let the flavors combine. Add whole milk, potatoes and fish sausages and simmer over low heat about 20 minutes or until the potatoes are tender. Add whitefish chunks to the chowder mixture and continue to cook until the fish is thoroughly warm, about 2 minutes. Adjust seasonings to taste, adding salt if desired.

Transfer chowder to serving bowls and garnish with crispy bacon pieces and chives.

Makes 6 servings.

CIDER-ROASTED LAMB LEG

1 partially boned lamb leg, about 4½ pounds
4 shallots, peeled and coarsely chopped
4 cloves garlic, peeled and smashed
4 fresh rosemary sprigs
2 cups Suttons Bay Tandem Cider
½ cup cider vinegar
6 hard Michigan apples, cored and quartered

PREPARATION: Let lamb come to room temperature, about 45 minutes, before searing the meat on the stove. Adjust oven rack to lower middle position and heat oven to 300 degrees.

Do not remove the netting around lamb until carving. Heat a Dutch oven or heavy-bottomed, sturdy skillet over medium-high heat until very hot. Spray pan with nonstick cooking spray and sear lamb on all sides until browned, about 8 minutes total. Transfer lamb to a small roasting pan. Reduce heat to the hot Dutch oven/skillet and sauté shallots, garlic, and rosemary 2 minutes. Add shallot mixture to roasting pan, along with hard cider and cider vinegar. Season with ground pepper; do not salt until the lamb is resting.

Roast until an instant-read thermometer registers 135 degrees for medium-rare, about 1 hour and 30 minutes. Roasting time depends on lamb size, but aim for roast-ing about 20-22 minutes per pound. Start checking the temperature about 30 minutes before estimated cooking time. Remove from oven before internal temperature hits 145 degrees, because the lamb will continue to cook 5 additional degrees once removed from the oven.

Gently transfer to a cutting board, cover with aluminum foil and let rest for 10 to 15 minutes to allow juices to redistribute. To make a pan gravy, strain the liquid (reserving the shallots, if desired), return to pan, add apples and reduce liquid and simmer apples until crunchy-tender, about 5 to 8 minutes. Carve lamb into ½-inch slices and serve with pan gravy with shallots and apples.

Makes 8 servings.

BIG JIM'S MEATBALLS WITH SPAGHETTI

MEATBALLS

2 pounds ground chuck, preferably grass-fed and organic
1 pound bulk Italian sausage, casing removed
½ cup freshly grated Parmesan cheese
1 large egg
1 medium onion, finely chopped
2 cloves garlic, peeled and finely minced
2 tablespoons chopped fresh leafy green herb, such as parsley, oregano, marjoram
Ground black pepper
¾ cup to 1 cup cracker crumbs

SAUCE

2 tablespoons olive oil
1 large onion, finely chopped
(1 carrot, peeled and grated; 1 bell pepper, seeded and diced: optional)
2 cloves garlic, finely minced
2 (28-ounce) cans organic diced tomatoes
2 (14.5-ounce) cans organic crushed fire-roasted tomatoes
2 tablespoons tomato paste
½ cup red wine
2 teaspoons granulated sugar
½ cup finely chopped fresh parsley
2 tablespoons finely chopped fresh basil leaves
2 pounds whole-wheat spaghetti

PREPARATION: Line a shallow baking pan with aluminum foil; lightly spray with cooking spray. Heat oven to 350 degrees.

In a large bowl, combine ground beef, pork sausage, Parmesan cheese, egg, onion, garlic, chopped fresh herbs, ground pepper, and cracker crumbs. With wet hands, combine until evenly mixed. Shape mixture into 1½-inch balls. You should be able to form about 28. Place meatballs on prepared pan and bake for 20 minutes until browned and cooked nearly through. Transfer to paper towel-lined baking sheet to drain.

For the sauce, in a sturdy stockpot, warm olive oil and sauté onions (and carrot and bell pepper) until soft and golden; do not let brown. Add garlic and sauté another minute. Add tomatoes with juices, paste, red wine, and sugar; bring to a simmer and let sauce thicken for 45 minutes. Stir in parsley and basil, season with salt and pepper to taste and continue simmering another 5 minutes.

Meanwhile, cook pasta in boiling salted water until al dente, drain and divide among serving plates. Top with sauce and meatballs. Serve with freshly grated Parmesan cheese, if desired.

Makes 8 to 10 servings (with about 28 meatballs.)

Vegtable Frittata

1 each gold flesh potato, small sweet potato, half a winter squash (seeded), cut vegetable into large chunks
2 tablespoons extra-virgin olive oil, divided
1 large sweet onion, cut into 1-inch pieces
1 red bell pepper, seeded and cut into 1-inch pieces
Handful of chopped spinach, arugula, or your favorite hearty greens. Toss in as many roasted vegetables that will fit in the pan and continue to cook.

EGG MIX
8 eggs
½ cup full-fat milk or half-and-half
½ cup freshly grated cheese (Parmesan, Cheddar, or Provolone)
Sea salt and freshly ground pepper
2 tablespoons freshly shredded basil, tarragon or sage

PREPARATION: Heat oven to 350 degrees. Place potato and sweet potato and half of the winter squash on a baking tray, drizzle with one tablespoon of oil and toss to coat. Bake for 30 minutes until crunchy tender.

Meanwhile, generously oil or butter an oven-proof 10-inch skillet, sauté the onions and bell pepper, until translucent, on a medium-low heat. Add spinach and stir until wilted. Toss in roasted vegetables and continue to cook.

In a large mixing bowl, add eggs, milk or half-and-half, cheese, salt, pepper, and herbs.

Whisk until fully incorporated. Pour egg mixture over vegetables. On stovetop, cook the frittata for about 3 to 4 minutes, until frittata begins to set around the edges. Place in oven and bake 25 to 30 minutes until golden brown. Remove from oven, run a knife around the edge of the frittata to loosen. Allow to stand 5 minutes before slicing and serving.

Makes 8 servings.

Zingerman's Roadhouse Macaroni and Three Peppercorn Goat Cheese

MACARONI

Coarse sea salt
1 pound macaroni
2 tablespoons butter
¼ cup diced onion
1 bay leaf
2 tablespoons all-purpose flour
1½ cups whole milk
¼ cup heavy cream
1 teaspoon Dijon mustard
2 cups fresh goat cheese
¾ cup chopped roasted red peppers
2 teaspoons freshly and coarsely ground black pepper-corns, plus more to taste
1 teaspoon freshly and coarsely ground white pepper-corns
1 teaspoon freshly and coarsely ground green peppercorns

AGED CHELSEA ROUNDS

4 ounces aged Chelsea goat cheese, cut into 4 rounds
1 large egg
2 tablespoons whole milk
1 cup bread crumbs
1 tablespoon butter for frying. (Fry the Chelsea rounds just before serving, so have ingredients ready.)

PREPARATION: Bring a large pot of water to a boil. Add 1 to 2 tablespoons salt and the pasta and stir well. Cook for about 13 minutes, until the pasta is done. Drain it and set it aside.

Meanwhile, melt the butter for the sauce in a large, heavy-bottomed pot over medium-high heat (don't scorch the butter). Add the onion and bay leaf and sauté until the onion is soft, about 5 minutes. Remove the bay leaf. Add the flour, and cook for a minute or so, stirring constantly.

Slowly add the milk, a little at a time, stirring constantly to avoid lumping. When the flour and milk are completely combined, stir in the cream. Keep the mixture at a gentle simmer until it thickens, 2 to 3 minutes.

Reduce the heat to medium. Stir in the mustard, goat cheese, red peppers, peppercorns, and salt. Stir the drained pasta into the cheese sauce. Taste and adjust the seasonings if necessary. Cover and remove from heat.

To fry the goat cheese slices, melt the butter over moderately high heat in a heavy-bottomed skillet. Beat together 1 egg and 2 tablespoons whole milk to mae the egg wash. Coat each round with the egg wash, then completely coat in breadcrumbs. Fry the cheese, about one minute each side, until golden.

Serve each bowl of macaroni topped with more cheese.

Makes 4 servings.

GOAT CHEESE MOUSSE IN PARMESAN CRISPS

MOUSSE
6 ounces fresh goat cheese, at room temperature
5 tablespoons heavy whipping cream
1 tablespoon parsley
Salt and pepper to taste

PARMESAN CRISPS
12 tablespoons finely grated Parmesan Reggiano

LAVENDER HONEY
¼ cup honey
¼ cup water
1 tablespoon fresh lavender

PREPARATION: For the mousse, put goat cheese in a stand mixer and whip until creamy; add cream, parsley, salt, and pepper; whip until smooth and set aside.

Heat oven to 350 degrees. For the Parmesan crisps, using a sheet pan lined with parchment paper, place 2 tablespoons Parmesan on the pan and spread with your finger to create a circle about 2 ½ inches in diameter. Repeat until all Parmesan is used.

Bake in a 350-degree oven until a light golden color is achieved, about 6 to 10 minutes. Be sure not to overcook. Have an empty egg carton ready. Remove the pan from the oven and, using a spatula, remove the crisps one at a time. Mold them into the egg carton, creating free-form bowls. Set aside to cool and harden.

For the lavender honey: Put honey, water, and fresh lavender into a saucepan and bring to a boil, cooking for 2 to 3 minutes. Remove from heat, strain, allow to cool.

To assemble, place a small dollop of the mousse on the plate. Put the Parmesan crisp on the dollop to keep from sliding. Fill the crisp with the mousse.

As an option, top with slices of fruit (such as peaches and plums) and watercress (about ½ cup) and drizzle with the honey.

Makes 6 goat cheese-Parmesan crisps.

From Jason Moniz, executive chef at Locavore Restaurant in San Francisco, California. Jason is the son of goat farmer Barbara Jenness of Dancing Goat Creamery in Byron Township, Michigan.

Julee Rosso's Raspberry Blueberry Bread Pudding and Vanilla Sauce

3 cups (1-inch) bread cubes, preferably French

10 tablespoons (1¼ sticks) unsalted butter, divided

5 cups heavy whipping cream, divided

½ cup granulated sugar, plus 2 tablespoons, divided

¼ teaspoon salt

6 large eggs

2 cups blueberries

1 cup raspberries

PREPARATION: Position rack in middle of the oven and heat to 350 degrees. Place bread cubes on baking sheet and toast until lightly brown, for about 12 minutes. Let cool. Generously butter (2 tablespoons) a 9-by-13-inch baking dish. Place the bread cubes in the dish.

In a medium bowl, whisk together 3 cups cream, ¼ cup sugar, ¼ teaspoon salt, and the eggs. Evenly distribute the berries over the bread cubes and pour the egg mixture over all. If necessary, re-submerge the berries gently. Sprinkle with 2 tablespoons sugar. Set aside for 15 minutes before baking. Bake 35-40 minutes, until golden brown and a knife inserted in the middle comes out clean.

Meanwhile, in a heavy saucepan, melt the remaining ¼ cup sugar, 2 cups heavy cream, and 8 tablespoons butter. Cook over medium high temperature, whisking occasionally to incorporate the melting butter into the cream. Do not let butter separate or the sauce will not work. Quickly bring to a boil, stirring occasionally, then turn heat down and continue cooking at a low boil (with periodic bubbles breaking the surface) and whisking occasionally so it doesn't burn on the bottom. Cook about 30 minutes, until the sauce thickens. Serve warm over squares of bread pudding.

Makes 12 servings.

Summertime Marinara Sauce

2½ pounds fresh ripe summer plum or heirloom tomatoes, coarsely chopped.

¼ cup of olive oil

2 large sweet onions, coarsely chopped

6 large cloves garlic, peeled and minced

1 teaspoon crushed red pepper flakes, optional

Sea or kosher salt and freshly ground black pepper

3 tablespoons of tomato paste, optional

Freshly grated Parmesan cheese

Handful fresh basil leaves, chopped

PREPARATION: In a sturdy stockpot, on medium heat, add the olive oil and heat until it shimmers but does not smoke. Add onions and garlic and sauté until they are tender, translucent and sweet-smelling, about 12 minutes. Do not let them brown— reduce heat if necessary. Add the tomatoes, season with salt and pepper and bring to a low boil. To balance the flavor and thicken the sauce, add 3 tablespoons of tomato paste and a pinch of granulated sugar to the tomatoes. Right away, reduce heat simmer for about 25-35 minutes. Though the tomatoes will break up some, don't overcook them, so when they have softly broken down, remove from heat. Stir in fresh herbs.

Makes enough for 4 to 6 servings with hot pasta.

Jaye and Terri's Garden Pesto

Up to ⅓ cup extra virgin olive oil

1½ cups fresh baby spinach, stems removed

¾ cups fresh basil leaves

½ cup pine nuts or walnuts, preferably toasted

4 ounces Parmesan cheese, freshly grated

2 medium cloves garlic, peeled

PREPARATION: To prepare in a food processor bowl, combine 2 tablespoons olive oil, spinach, basil, pine nuts or walnuts, cheese and garlic. Cover and process until smooth, stopping processor and scraping sides as necessary. Drizzle in remaining olive oil until mixture is smooth. Makes about 1-¾ cups.

OVEN ROASTED TOMATOES

2½ pounds summer-ripened plum or heirloom tomatoes

2 to 4 tablespoons olive oil

6 to 8 cloves garlic, peeled and minced, optional

1 Sea salt and freshly ground black pepper

½ cup chopped fresh basil leaves, for sprinkling

PREPARATION: Heat oven to 300 degrees. Line a rimmed baking tray with parchment paper. In a mixing bowl, slice plum tomatoes in half, lengthwise, or quarter round tomatoes. Toss the tomatoes with olive oil and minced garlic, coating thoroughly. Place them, cut side up on the baking tray. Season with sea salt and freshly ground black pepper. Roast for 2 to 2½ hours, checking periodically. The tomatoes should be shrunken like dried apricots but still retain their brilliant red and shape after cooking. Don't let them blacken or they will taste bitter. Sprinkle with chopped fresh basil and let cool slightly. Before freezing, pinch off the skin, which should easily slip off. Roasted tomatoes will keep in an airtight container in the refrigerator for one week or in the freezer for up to six months. Bring to room temperature before using.

FOR ROASTED TOMATO SOUP: Transfer oven-roasted tomatoes to a large stockpot. Add 3 cups chicken stock and 2 bay leaves; bring to a boil, reduce heat and simmer for 15 to 20 minutes or until liquid has reduced by a third. In batches, puree in the blender or with an immersion blender, until smooth. Return soup to low heat, add ½ cup basil if you didn't sprinkle it on the tomatoes already. Stir in ½ cup heavy cream and adjust consistency with chicken stock, if necessary. Season to taste with salt and freshly ground black pepper.

Makes 4 to 6 servings.

Rob Burdick's Roasted Winter Squash Halves

2 winter squash, halved length-wise

4 teaspoons unsalted butter, at room temperature

Salt and pepper to taste

Cherry Republic Ambassador Mix, finely chopped

Pure maple syrup for drizzling

PREPARATION: Adjust an oven rack to the lower middle position and heat oven to 375 degrees.

Scoop the seeds and stringy pulp out of the squash cavities and discard. Place them cut side down on two 13-by-9-inch baking dishes. Add enough water to measure ½-inch in each dish. Bake for about 45 minutes until the squash is nearly tender when pierced with a fork. Remove squash from the oven and turn cut-side up.

Score the squash so the butter and syrup penetrates into the meat. Salt and pepper to taste. To each half, add 1 teaspoon butter, 2 tablespoons cherry mix, and drizzle of maple syrup. Return to oven and roast until the squash begins to caramelize, about 10 minutes.

Remove from oven and serve immediately.

Makes 4 servings.

Eggplant Caponata

1 small onion

1 zucchini

1 eggplant

1 red bell pepper

1 green bell pepper

2 cloves garlic, peeled and minced

½ pound heiloom tomatoes

2 tablespoons fresh basil leaves, shredded

1 tablespoon chopped fresh parsley

¼ cup golden raisins, plumped in hot water and drained

2 tablespoons extra virgin olive oil

1 tablespoon white wine vinegar

2 tablespoons toasted pine nuts

Sea salt and freshly ground pepper

PREPARATION: The key to a good caponata is to cut everything the same size and cook each part individually so nothing is overcooked. Cut your veggies into a medium dice. Heat oil in a skillet and fry each veggie in turn, then remove from pan and add to a big bowl. Season each veggie with salt and pepper as you are cooking it. Add the garlic to the last vegtable you cook, and cook for one minute. Don't cook the tomatoes, just add those in raw. Stir in the herbs, raisins, olive oil, vingar and pine nuts. Check seasoning again, and add more salt and pepper if necessary. Serve this at room temperature.

Makes 10 servings.

STONE HOUSE THREE CHEESE-TOMATO SANDWICHES

1 loaf ciabatta bread, sliced

Olive oil for spreading

About ½ cup basil pesto, preferably homemade

8 slices aged Swiss cheese

1 round fresh mozzarella cheese

2 large beefsteak tomatoes, thinly sliced

8 slices aged Cheddar cheese

PREPARATION: Heat gas grill to medium. Cut loaf of ciabatta bread horizontally. Spread a thin layer of olive oil on top and bottom of bread so it does not stick to grill. Spread a thin layer of pesto on bread and top with Swiss, mozzarella, and tomato slices. Finish with cheddar and cover with top of ciabatta. Repeat until out of ingredients. Grill indirect, flipping once, till lightly brown and cheese is melted.

Makes 8 sandwiches.

From Stone House Bread in Leland, Michigan

CAFÉ MUSE BRAISED SHORT RIBS

4 to 5 pounds short ribs, preferably boneless

1 teaspoon sea salt

¼ teaspoon freshly cracked pepper

2 tablespoons olive oil

3 shallots, peeled and diced

6 cloves garlic, peeled and chopped

1 cup Arcturos' Pinot Noir

3 large tomatoes, with seeds removed and diced

Fresh thyme sprigs, tied together with string

Large heavy bottomed sauté pan

Roaster large enough to hold the meat

PREPARATION: Heat oven to 350 degrees. Season the meat on both sides with salt and pepper. Heat the sauté pan over high. Add oil, followed by the short ribs. Brown ribs well on both sides. If the pan is small, brown in stages. Once the meat is browned, transfer to roaster.

In the sauté pan, add the shallots, then the garlic. Sweat the mixture under low heat for about a minute, being careful not to burn. Then deglaze the pan with the red wine and add tomatoes. Deglazing is the technique that allows you to use the caramelized bits of meat and fat that remain in the pan to help create sauce. Throw in the thyme and pour over the ribs. Make sure meat is covered by the tomato mixture. Loosely cover roaster with parchment paper or a lid. Do not use aluminum foil because the acids will react to it.

Cook in the oven until tender—about 2 to 2½ hours. Transfer to a container large enough to accommodate and refrigerate overnight. The next day, remove fat around the top. Slowly reheat in a 350 degree oven and serve. Makes 6 to 8 servings.

Ricotta gnocchi with tomatoes and rosemary

GNOCCHI

1 (16-ounce) container ricotta cheese, drain overnight if watery

Enough flour to fill ricotta container

1 egg

1 teaspoon fine sea salt

Flour for rolling

PAN SAUCE

1 teaspoon olive oil

1 shallot, peeled and diced

2 to 3 garlic cloves, peeled and chopped

¼ cup Chateau Fontaine Chardonnay

1 cup diced tomatoes

½ cup vegetable or chicken stock

½ teaspoon fresh rosemary

¼ cup shredded Parmesan cheese

¼ cup shredded Asiago cheese

Salt and pepper to taste

PREPARATION: To make the gnocchi, in a large bowl, place flour, ricotta, egg, and salt. Mix with hands until well-incorporated. The dough should be sticky but workable. Wrap dough in plastic wrap. Let dough sit in the refrigerator for 15 minutes to relax.

Remove dough from refrigerator. Lightly flour work surface. Cut a quarter of the dough and rewrap the rest. Lightly flour hands and dough. Roll out dough into log the thickness of a thumb. Cut dough segments into ¾-inch pieces. Once all the dough is cut, gently toss with flour to prevent sticking. On a sheet tray small enough to fit flat in the refrigerator, create one layer of pasta and refrigerate. Repeat with each quarter of dough. Use waxed or parchment paper between each layer of gnocchi. At this point, gnocchi may be cooked or frozen for later use.

—To freeze the dough, place in the freezer, making sure the gnocchi do not touch each other. Allow the dough to freeze completely and transfer to freezer bags.

— To cook the dough, use a large pot of lightly salted boiling water, drop in gnocchi. Stir gently to prevent the pasta from sticking. Once the gnocchi begins to float to the top, cook for another minute or two. Drain and toss with sauce.

—To make the pan sauce, in a sauté pan over medium heat, add olive oil, shallots, and garlic. Sauté for a minute, stirring. Add wine, followed by tomatoes and stock. Simmer for 3 to 4 minutes to reduce. Add cooked gnocchi and rosemary. Sprinkle in cheeses and toss until cheeses are melted. Season with sea salt and freshly cracked pepper.

Royal Oak spinach salad

BALSAMIC VINAIGRETTE

One-third-cup balsamic vinegar

1 teaspoon honey

1 teaspoon whole-grain mustard

1 cup extra-virgin olive oil

Sea salt and freshly cracked pepper to taste

SALAD

½ pound spinach

½ cup pecans

½ cup dried Traverse City cherries

½ cup crumbled Gorgonzola cheese

PREPARATION: To make vinaigrette, place the vinegar, honey, mustard, and ½ teaspoon salt in a blender. Pulse a few times to dissolve the salt and combine the ingredients. With the blender running, slowly pour in the olive oil. Once all the oil is added, continue to run the blender for another 30 seconds. Taste and add salt and pepper.

To make salad greens, wash greens and dry well. In a large bowl, toss the spinach with the vinaigrette. Plate up and top with pecans, cherries, and gorgonzola.

Index

A

American Agri-Women organization 33

American Cheese Society 110

American Grown Goodness 33

Ann Arbor Farmers Market 50, 138, 149

Ann Arbor HomeGrown Festival 50, 149

Apples

  Baldwin 71

  Calville Blancs 70

  Duchess of Oldenburg 72

  Esopus Spitzenburg 70

  Green New Pippen 70

  Ingrid Marie 72

  Pumpkin Sweet, 72

  Roxbury russet 70

  Sheep's nose 71

  Snow White 50, 72

  The Lady 71

  Tolman's Sweet 70

  Turkish Kandel Sinep 72

  Wagoner 71

  Westfield Seek-No-Further 72

  Yellow Newtown Pippin 72

  Zestar 67

Apple Valley 102

Araucana hens 15

Arbogast-Carlson Farm 58

Art of the Table 164

Asparagus 26, 27, 187, 188

Asparagus Festival 27

Avalon International Bread 162

B

Bay Mills Indian Community 81

Beans-to-chocolate Bars 178

Big Jim's Meatballs with Spaghetti 202

Big Stone Bay Fishery 88

Black-eyed peas with Collard Greens and Tomato Broth 192

Black Angus 33

Blackberry

  Apache 67

Blackhawk 169

Black Star Farms 112, 180

Blueberries
  Bluecrop 34
  Bluejay 34
  Blueray 52
  Duke 34
  Elliott 34
  Jersey 34, 52
  Rubel 34

Boetsma 169

Boeve Farm 169

Bortell's Fish Shack 86

Brother Nature 25, 45, 46, 47, 62, 167

Building Alliances for Local Living Economies 10

Byron Meats 140

C

Café Muse, 159, 170

Calder Dairy 161

Carbon's Golden Malted 170

Centennial Cranberry Farm 60

Cheboygan Farmers Market 142

Cheese
  Chevre 109
  Dancing Goat chevre 110
  Pesto chevre 111
  Phocas 106
  Raclette 112

Chef Matt Pietsch 168

Chef Myles Anton 167

Cherry Capital Foods 35

Cherry Point Farm and Market 150

Chestnuts 75

Christmas Cove 70

Cisela Farm 169

Community Supported Agriculture 34, 37, 46

Corktown 162

Coveyou Scenic Farm 138

Cows
  Belted Galloways 128
  Jersey 105, 115
  Shaggy Scottish Highlanders 128
  Texas Longhorns 128

Cowslip 105, 118

Cranberries
  Early Blacks 60
  Howes 60

Crane's Orchard 171

Crane Dance Farm 121, 124

Crestwick Farms 140, 150, 169

Crooked Creek Dairy 170

Culinary Escapes 159

D

D-Town Farm 48, 49

Dancing Goat Creamery 109, 118

DeGrandchamps Farm 60

Dequindre Cut Trail Mix Cookies 162

Detroit Black Community Food Security Farm 47

Dunneback 28-33, 62

E

Easter Egger 15

Eastern Market 21, 47, 49, 75, 138, 144-148

Eater's Guild Farm 37, 62

Ebels Family Center 131

Eco-Acres 169

Eggplant

　Fairytale 141

　Gretel 141

　Hansel 141

Evergreen Lanes Creamery 21, 169

F

FarmBoy FlapJack 149

Farm Country Cheese Store 118

Farnsworth Family Farm 162

Farrell Fruit 149

Figs

　Black Spanish 15

　Peter's Honey 15

　Vern's Brown Turkey 15

Forest Hills Foods 102

Friske Orchard 167

Fulton Street Farmers Market 43, 57, 83, 108, 138, 150, 154

Funny Farm Organics 150

G

Gallagher Centennial Farm 121, 129-131, 134

Goats

　Alpine 37, 109

　Nubian 15, 37, 40

　Golden River Orchards 143

Grand Central Station 102

Grand Marais Farmers Market 138

Grand River Grocery 102, 180

Grand Traverse Band of Ottawa and Chippewa Indians 81

Grand Traverse Regional Land Conservancy, 12

Grand Traverse Resort and Spa 6, 158-159

Grand Valley State University 9, 12, 111

Grapes

　Hemrod 67

Grassfield's Cheese 119

Greening of Detroit 44, 49, 148

　Grown in Detroit 49, 62, 146, 148

Green Meadow Dairy 161

Green Toe Gardens Honey 173

Groundswell CSA Farm 150

H

Harvest Health 102

Hermann's Bakery 159, 164

Hilhof Dairy 97, 101, 118, 140

Hogs

  Guinea 129

J

Jam Lady 174-176

Jampot 176-178

Jennings Brothers Stone-Ground Grains, 57

John Cross Fisheries 89, 90

Joy Southfield Farmers Market 49

K

Kellogg Foundation 49

Kilcherman's Christmas Cove Farm 70-72, 78

King's Fish Market 83, 94

King's Mill 60, 108

Kingma's Market 98, 102

Kismet Organics 78, 187, 198

Koeze Cream-Nut 140

L

L&J Meat Market 130

L.H. Piggott and Girls Family Farm, 138, 148, 154

Lake Street Café 143

Land of Goshen 129, 143, 167

Latitudes Cranberry Bean Hummus 187, 192

Learn Great Foods 158

Leelanau Cellars 114

Leelanau Cheese Co. 112, 114, 119

Legs Inn 87, 94

Leslie Science & Nature Center and County Farm Park 50

Light of Day Organics 53-54, 62, 143

Little Red Rooster Bakery 104, 108, 150

Local First 10

Lunasa 62-63, 138, 150

M

Mackinac Straits Fish Company 83, 152

Majszak Farm 167

Mallory's Busy Beehive 171

Maple Hill Farms 67

Maple Syrup

  Maple Butter 77

  Maple Cream 77

 Martha's Vineyard 102

 McManus Brothers 68

Mesick Morel Festival 25

Michigan Bean Commission 58

Michigan Cheese Makers Cooperative 98, 118

Michigan Chestnut Growers Inc 75

Michigan Higher Education Land Policy Consortium 9

Michigan Organic Farm Alliance 37

Mill Pond 150

Mizuma 46

Mooville Creamery 151

Motor City Brewing Works 45

Mudgie's Deli 47

Mud Lake Farm 150, 169

N

Native Americans 90, 124

North American Farmers' Direct Marketing Association, 30

Northwest Detroit Farmers Market, 49

Nourish 164

O

Old Mission Peninsula 12, 68, 129, 158

Old Pine Farm 121, 127-129, 134

Oleson Markets 132

Oryana Natural Foods Market 129, 138, 143-144, 154

Oven-Roasted Tomatoes 209

P

Palazzolo's Artisan Gelato and Sorbetto 140, 169, 171-172, 184

Patricia's Chocolate 180

Peaches

  Flamin' Fury 66, 67

  Peento 67

  Redhavens 67

  Stellar 67

Pears

  Anjou 73

  Barlett 73

  Clapp's Favorite 21, 73

  Comice 73

  Eldorado 73

  Seckel 73

Pleasant Hill Farm 34-36, 62

Pleasanton Brick Oven Bakery 143, 163, 184

Project Grow 49-50, 52, 62

Purslane 46, 123

R

Rapid Growth Media 42

Ricotta Gnocchi with Tomatoes and Rosemary 212

Roasted Pear Sauce 197

Royal Oak Spinach Salad 213

Russ Latchaw 169

S

S&S Lamb 151

Salt of the Earth 140, 168-169, 184

Sharon's Old-Fashioned Canned Goods 140

Sheep

  Navajo Churros 129

  Tunis 129

Shetler's Dairy 98, 118, 143, 167

Simmons Family Farms 149

Slow Food 6, 22, 106, 108, 11, 127, 149

Sobe Meats 102, 165

Spirit Farms 47

Stone House Breads 162-163, 211

Straathofs 98, 101

Strawberries

  All-star 29

  Darsalect 29

  Earliglows 29

  Everbearing 29

  Honeye 29

  Jewels 29

Summertime Market 138, 139, 154

Sun Ra Farms 171

Superior Fish Shop 83

Superior Seafood Market 85, 159

T

The Cook's House 180

The Grand Rapids Press 6, 9, 12, 17, 98

The Lubbers 104-106, 108

The Michigan Land Resource Project 11

The Ridge 30

Tilling-to-Table 106

Tomatoes

  Black Zebra 50

  Brandywine 50, 167

  Garden Peach 50

  Green Zebra 21, 50, 167

  Italian Costoluto Genovese 50

  Jimbo 50

  Principe Borghese 50

  Roma 53

  Snow White 50, 72

  West Virginia Hillbilly 50

Trattoria Stella 129, 167

Trillium Haven 26, 41-43, 46, 62, 193

U

United States Bean Council 59

V

Vang Farm 146-147

Visser Farm 151

W

Wayne State University Farmers Market 47, 49

Wealthy Street Bakery 164

Werp Farms 159, 170

West Michigan Cooperative 138, 150, 154

Westwind Milling 56-57, 63

Whitefish Chowder 199

Winchester at Wealthy 165-166

Woodbridge Pub 166-167, 184

Z

Zingerman's Bakehouse 6, 159, 184

Zingerman's Deli 146, 149, 159, 161

Zingerman's Roadhouse 160

Zingerman's Roadhouse Macaroni and Goat Cheese 204